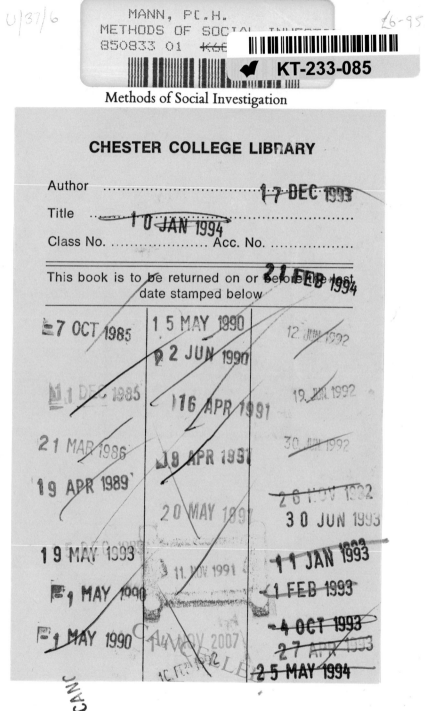

Methods of
Social Investigation

PETER H. MANN

Basil Blackwell

© Peter H. Mann 1968, 1985

First published 1968 as *Methods of Sociological Enquiry*
Second edition 1985

Basil Blackwell Ltd
108 Cowley Road, Oxford OX4 1JF, UK

Basil Blackwell Inc.
432 Park Avenue South, Suite 1505,
New York, NY 10016, USA

British Library Cataloguing in Publication Data

Mann, Peter H.
  Methods of social investigation.— 2nd ed.
  1. Social sciences—Research
  I. Title II. Mann, Peter H. Methods of
  sociological enquiry
  300'.72   H62
  ISBN 0—631—14408—0
  ISBN 0—631—14019—0 (Pbk.)

Library of Congress Cataloging in Publication Data

Mann, Peter H.
  Methods of social investigation.
  Rev. ed. of: Methods of sociological enquiry. 1968.
  Bibliography: p.
  Includes index
  1. Sociology—Research. 2. Sociology—Methodology.
  I. Mann, Peter H. Methods of Sociological enquiry.
  II. Title.
  HM48.M35 1985 301'.072   84—28322
  ISBN 0—631—14408—0
  ISBN 0—631—14019—0 (pbk.)

Typeset by Cambrian Typesetters, Frimley, Surrey
Printed in Great Britain by Billing & Sons Ltd., Worcester

Contents

Preface to the Second Edition

The first edition of this book was published in 1968 and the fact that it has since gone into several impressions and has been translated into Portuguese for South American countries, and also into Japanese, must say something about its popularity.

I know from several students in disciplines outside sociology itself that it has been useful to people in education, librarianship, health studies and other fields where social investigation is carried out. The fact that this elementary introduction to *doing* research (rather than just talking about it) has helped so many people gives me great pleasure. When I was a very young and inexperienced junior research assistant at Liverpool University my first graduate job entailed working for a very experienced researcher, Denis Chapman, to whom I have always felt that I was 'apprenticed' for two years. He taught me a great deal about the basics of field research and that one must earn the right to theorize through collecting good evidence to test one's case. I have never ceased to be grateful for that introduction to research work.

Denis Chapman also taught me that sociology did not have to be obscured by impenetrable jargon and consequently I have always tried to write so that non-specialists can understand me. This small book is intended for the student (of any age or status) who wants to learn how to start doing social research. I have tried in it to get to the root of things and to show that, demanding though objective research is, it can nevertheless be exciting and even fun. I believe that good social investigation takes the researcher close to people but, at the same time, the researcher must learn to keep his distance emotionally. This is not an easy balance to achieve but it must be sought just the same.

I hope, in the pages which follow, that my own enjoyment in social research will come through to the reader. Really good research is immensely satisfying and fully justifies the preparations needed. This basic text will, I hope, both guide and encourage.

Peter H. Mann
Loughborough University

1

The Study of Social Behaviour

All the social sciences are concerned, in one way or another, with the study of social behaviour. Economics, political theory, social anthropology, human geography, social psychology and several other disciplines all have their own particular perspectives on the study of human beings and how they behave towards each other. Sociology, one of whose founders had hopes of it becoming 'the queen of the social sciences' is, as one early British sociologist described it, 'In the broadest sense . . . the study of human interactions and interrelations, their conditions and consequences'. There must by now be hundreds of definitions of sociology but this one, by Morris Ginsberg,[1] will suffice for the moment as it enables us to consider what we are involved in when we try to study social behaviour. In this chapter we shall consider the background to social research, looking particularly at sociology, since it is in many ways the most general of the social sciences, and consider how one can go about studying social behaviour in a scientific manner.

Sociology is about the conditions and consequences of social interaction and interrelationships. It is therefore about the structure of society and the effects on social life of certain structures. Conversely it must also be about the effects of social life, especially changing social life, on the structures. Sociology is about group life and deals with groups as groups — from small groups, such as families or friends, right the way through to whole societies. Social research, therefore, is about social behaviour, rather than individual behaviour, and it seeks social explanations of behaviour.

We are all members of groups — dozens and dozens of groups of all kinds. Perhaps we do not often think about these memberships when we limit our concept of the group to such obvious ones as our family, our workplace, perhaps our church and our political party. But if we widen the idea of 'group' to include our membership of insurance companies, of the Automobile Association, of our nation state and even of NATO, then we find ourselves members of almost limitless numbers of groups. Clearly, to include both one's football supporters club and one's nation state under the same heading of 'group' is to use the term in a very broad sense indeed and so sociology, in particular among the social sciences, concerns itself with devising new and better ways of studying and classifying social interaction with a view to the better understanding of its structures and its processes. 'Primary' and 'secondary' groups are two traditional ways of distinguishing between types of groups.

Social interaction, with all the many ways in which it can be manifested, is an extremely complicated field for investigation. To claim for the subject of sociology that it is a *scientific* study of society might well seem to be claiming too much. No sensible sociologist would ever deny that to *try* to study society scientifically is difficult. Not only is the field for study very complex, but also the sociologist, as a human being, is to some extent or other a part of it, with all his or her personal values, biases and prejudices. What is important is that social researchers should make the attempt to eradicate their preconceptions and prejudices; otherwise the research will be no more than a personal statement which readers cannot trust.

The big problem is to know how and where to start on a scientific approach to the study of social behaviour. Sadly, some people have turned their faces against the difficult task of striving for objectivity and seem to think that if they begin by saying they are biased towards one particular viewpoint then this will disarm their critics. This is a naive belief to hold; one would be astonished to hear a judge in a law court declaring his bias against a defendant and then expecting the court to accept his judgement. It will be a constant theme in this book that personal bias in social research is a serious problem, so the research should try hard to overcome it, not try to make a virtue of it.

Where then should the researcher start in this daunting task? Some critics of the social sciences, and especially of sociology, have claimed that there is too much stating of the obvious. Such criticisms usually take the line that we are all of us members of society, we are all aware of what goes on around us and we all understand reasonably well what is happening to us. We do not need pretentious social research projects costing thousands of pounds and wrapped up in fancy jargon to tell us what we know already. Jargon can, to some degree, make any simple statement look erudite until one strips the verbiage off; then it can look like a simple statement, such as 'the more we are together, the merrier we shall be.'

Other critics of social research, however, feel that sociologists are wasting their time trying to explain the inexplicable. For these critics human behaviour is far too complex to be amenable to scientific explorations. Human motivations cannot be analysed by computers and statistical tables. The poor record of sociologists as predictors of social behaviour is sometimes cited to show how rarely they have forecast race riots or revolutions and if sociologists know so much about deviant behaivour why does the crime rate keep on rising? There is too, these days, a certain dislike among many people, which is quite understandable, of social scientists' attempts to measure behaviour, since this seems to dehumanize people. After, or during, general elections there is usually some criticism of public opinion polls which some people (usually on the losing side) feel can influence people's behaviour. Certainly there are critics too of the popularity ratings for pop records and television programmes which tend to give people the impression that everything today is measured and only the majority counts. So there is resistance both to the attempts to study society objectively and also to some of the results they produce.

Obviously there are some valid points in all these criticisms. Some points can be refuted and indeed must be refuted if the social sciences are to operate as scientific disciplines rather than as ideological propaganda machines. The critics who say that the workings of society are obvious to us all must be asked how systematic is their understanding of society? To take just one example: we are all of us aware that there are social differentiations in our society, but how many of us would have the temerity to claim that we really understand how our class system works? As individuals we take part in only a minute segment of the total social life of our society and we would be stupid to claim that our own limited experience is adequate for us to generalize upon.

The critics who argue that life is too complex to generalize upon are proved wrong every moment of the day. If life were utterly complex it would be unliveable — no one would know what to do next. Everyday life is, in fact, extremely ordered, at times even to the point of boredom. Every day when we wake up we make assumptions, which are nearly always correct, about the behaviour of the employees in the major utilities such as water, electricity, gas, transport, communications, newspapers and so on. As we drive to work we do not (I hope) agonize about whether other road users will today continue to drive on the left as we observed they did yesterday. For the most part ordinary social behaviour is predictable because we subscribe to certain codes of behaviour which are for the benefit of us all. When we find ourselves without, say, our newspapers, because of yet another strike, then our predictions are proved wrong and we have to make adjustments. But for the most part the patterned behaviour of normal life gives a predictability which in turn gives security. It is the study of the repetitive patterns of social behaviour which lies at the heart of sociological research. The untypical or unique can then be seen in context.

All interaction between people, whether it is just between two people (say a courting couple) or between thousands of people (say at a pop festival) is based on mutual expectations about behaviour. The interaction which ensues from correct interpretation of expectations means that *prediction* is an important part of social life. Not only do we predict the behaviour of certain categories of people (such as postmen, newspaper boys and milkmen whom we expect to make deliveries to our homes) but we also make predictions about the behaviour of people with whom we have no personal contact at home. Every time we turn on a water tap, switch on the light or the gas fire, we are making predictions about the social behaviour of thousands of people who work in the public utilities. The chaos that is caused by strikes or by bad weather affecting public services only highlights how accustomed we are to our predictions being right rather than wrong.

So, in our prediction of social behaviour we are really saying to ourselves something along these lines: 'From my knowledge and experience of the society I live in I can predict with a quite high degree of accuracy that each day the public services will provide my home with water, gas, electricity and waste-disposal; that transport services by bus, train, aeroplane and ship will operate according to (or somewhere near!) the timetables they publish; that factories, offices, shops and public buildings will be open and operating between certain hours.' The list of these predictions can be endless, the more detailed we get. I suggest to the reader that you now pause to consider some simple examples of prediction from personal experience. For example, when you go to the public library, or the supermarket or to church, what sorts of predictions do you make about people's behaviour in these social settings? Then try to think of a social setting that might cause you some problems in predicting behaviour. Would you know how to conduct yourself if you were at, say, the Lord Mayor of London's banquet, a strip club in Soho, or on the floor of the Stock Exchange? If you can decide what your problems would be you are some way to seeing what you need to learn to conform.

It is important to realize that in the predictions referred to above we are not really concerned with the predicting of the behaviour of individual people. We do not predict that our neighbour John Smith will leave home at 8.15 a.m. to catch the 8.30 train to be in his office at 9 a.m. There will be many John Smiths who, for one reason or another, will not do so each day. Some of them will have died during the night, some will be ill, some on holiday, some will oversleep and be late for work, but in spite of these exceptions from normality we shall be able to predict with a high degree of accuracy for thousands of other people who have not deviated from their normal patterns of everyday behaviour. Our prediction then is a social prediction and it is not invalidated by there being some individual exceptions to it.

As can readily be seen, some social predictions are more likely to be accurate than others and it is through dressing up rather low-level predictions in fancy jargon that sociologists often incur the scorn of the 'common sense' critics. But there are many forms of prediction which can be expressed numerically with quite high degrees of accuracy which are, to some extent, 'common sense' and which no one would call pretentious. Actuarial predictions, for example, use detailed statistics to predict for the future and actuaries are highly skilled people who are highly rewarded for their skills in both the public and private sectors. The fact that actuaries predict accurately and quantitatively makes them very useful people. When we look at social trends we find predictions about the likelihood of marriages ending in divorce which are based on careful analysis of past data. It is then possible to forecast that certain categories of people who marry will be more 'at risk' than others. Of course, things might change (and overall population forecasting is very tricky), but for the most part society does not change radically overnight. Many people. in public services and in business, must make predictions about the future since their very jobs depend upon them. The marketing director who refused to predict the take-up of a new model of car would soon be out of a job. If his prediction is badly wrong he may be out of a job anyway, but no car company could operate without market predictions.

Most of the predictions mentioned so far have been of a quantitative sort. Predictions about public utilities and motor manufacturing may be interesting but would hardly seem to lie at the core of sociology itself. This is true, but it would be shortsighted not to look at the quantitative evidence that is available to the social scientist which he can use to help him see beyond the happenings of daily life. It is only recently in Britain that the wearing of crash helmets on motor cycles and the use of seat belts on the front seats of cars have been made compulsory. Statistical evidence on the use of seat belts has quickly shown what a reduction in fatalities and serious injuries the seat belt law brought about. Yet the resistance to this legislation was at one time very strong indeed and doubtless resistance to compulsory seat belts in the back seats of cars will continue. Cigarette smoking has been shown to be linked with lung cancer and all British cigarette packets must now carry a government warning. But cigarette companies are still free to advertise publicly (though not on television) and to sponsor a wide range of sports and other activities. A recent government enquiry into the eating habits of the British people would seem to advise that a change of diet (especially to fewer fats) could reduce ill health and deaths considerably, but commercial interests seem to be opposed to the publication of the report. In these three instances scientists of one sort or another have carefully studied quantitative data on what are essentially social aspects of human behaviour and have drawn certain conclusions from their evidence without fear or favour. The researches throw interesting light on the concept of 'freedom' even if it may mean freedom to injure or kill oneself and, as such, these studies should be of considerable interest to the student of society.

However, relevant though the study of accidents and ill health may be to the study of society it is less central to sociology itself than are more direct social indicators of what may be called 'social pathology'. In Britain there is a rich empirical tradition of studying poverty by means of social surveys. The earliest surveys, carried out by such groups as the Manchester Statistical Society and by public health pioneers such as Edwin Chadwick, all used the people themselves in the study of living conditions. Charles Booth and B. Seebohm Rowntree both left their mark on the study of poverty at the turn of the century,[2] when they tried to measure the extent of poverty in London and in York. Rowntree in particular is remembered for the attention he gave in his work to dietary factors and for his conceptualization of primary and secondary poverty and of the poverty cycle. In post-war years the work of Peter Townsend and his associates has completely altered the way that some social scientists now look at poverty.[3] Townsend's concept of relative deprivation changed the concept of poverty from one based on bare subsistence (necessary to keep a person fit enough for work) to a relative state in which the poor are now compared to more affluent groups in society and in which the poverty line is based on social security benefits. As the benefits increase so the poverty line moves up, and as poverty is always relative to this line (in fact 40 per cent above it), it follows that poverty defined in these terms can never be eradicated. The differences, then, between the concepts developed by Rowntree and Townsend are quite fundamental and neither is 'right' or 'wrong' — both are simply ways of looking at a particular social phenomenon.

Such definitions of social concepts only emphasize the importance in social research of formulating clear concepts which readers fully understand and of measuring as accurately as possible the incidence of certain types of social behaviour. When the definition has been standardized, then instances can be gathered together for analysis and, with varying degrees of accuracy, predictions may be made. The statistical projection over time is the most commonplace of this type.

But let us now consider another type of prediction. You, the reader, are asked to close your eyes and try to conjure up a mental picture of the inside of a prison. The prisoners are queueing for a meal. Do this now. Did you manage that all right? And did you imagine the prisoners to be men or women? I have done this little experiment many times with students and only on a couple of occasions, even with classes with half girls, have I had anyone say that they conjured up a mental picture of the inside of a women's prison. Apart from the satisfaction it gives me to be able to predict the students' behaviour so accurately, this little example shows how we tend to associate one phenomenon with another. Most prisoners *are* men anyway, so it is not surprising that we tend to think of prisons with men in them rather than women. We should be fairly safe too in predicting that next year the prisons will still be largely populated by men. If, next year, women formed the bulk of the prison population we should all be very surprised.

This simple example, linking masculinity with criminality, demonstrates an important aspect of social prediction. The attempt to link together characteristics is an important part of social investigation. Many stereotypes are about linked characteristics. The Scots are mean, the Welsh are musical, the Irish are stupid — these are music-hall stereotypes which no one really takes seriously. But stereotypes about Jews or black people can be nasty and dangerous. Years ago Montesquieu attempted to link social and psychological traits with various areas of the world. He thought of the people of northern Europe as tough and hardy because of their constant battle with the climate, whereas the people of the south, around the Mediterranean, were much softer because of their warm climate. Such geographical determinism is not accepted today by serious scholars, but many ordinary people still retain a certain north–south stereotype, ridiculous though it may be. When we think in such stereotyped ways we are associating factor A with factor B, with the idea that this association will, in some way, be explanatory. Yorkshiremen feel superior to people in the south of England because they come from the hardy north. Just why this makes them superior is not very clearly spelled out and so we see that stereotype correlations are often based on very poor conceptualization.

In serious social research there are innumerable attempts to link together two factors in an explanatory way. Do broken homes produce juvenile delinquents? Do middle-class children have higher educational success than working-class children? Are nationalized industries more prone to stikes than private sector ones? Is book reading predominantly a middle-class habit? Time and again the research question is put, either explicitly or implicitly, in terms of a correlation between factor A and factor B. Some of the postulated linkages may be on a grand scale, particularly when social scientists try to analyse and predict for whole societies over the course of history. Karl Marx said that 'the history of all hitherto existing society is the history of class struggles.' This indicates clearly enough the explanatory factor that Marx uses throughout his work and the type of prediction one may expect from him.

Linkages, then, can be expected to be found in all sorts of social researches, from problem families through to problem societies. Note that I am using the word linkages here rather than the more specific term correlation which suggests statistical links which can be tested by known formulae. There are important, indeed fundamental, differences between correlations and causal relationships and it is extremely dangerous to suggest that just because A is linked, even statistically, with B that A is necessarily the cause of B. One well-known example of this spurious correlation is the relationship between high temperatures in the summer and the increased consumption of ice-cream. One would have little difficulty in establishing such a correlation between two variables. One would also expect the correlation to lead to a causal explanation that the rising temperature causes people to consume more ice-cream. But why should one not put forward the hypothesis that the increasing consumption of ice-cream causes the temperature to rise? If our immediate reaction is, not surprisingly, that this is a stupid explanation, we have already gone beyond the correlation and made an alternative explanation from our prior knowledge of how the world and its inhabitants function. We know that no matter how many millions of people together licked ice-cream cornets they could not raise the temperature by a single degree. 'Common sense' tells us so. But common sense, as we call it, is derived from our knowledge of how things work.

When we come to research into social behaviour which affects people's relationships with each other, rather than with ice-cream, then the linking of social characteristics becomes more contentious. For example, sociologists use the concept of social class a great deal for the analysis of all sorts of social behaviour. Analysis of university students by the social class of their fathers shows that young people from middle-class families are statistically more likely to enter university than are young people from working-class families. There is, then, a correlation between university entry and social class and, obviously, entry is then seen to be in a causal relationship with social class. But university entry is normally based on the results of certain examinations and, particularly in the case of A levels or high-school examinations, the people who mark the papers know nothing about the social class of the candidates. So we now have to re-formulate the linkage to say that young people from middle-class homes do better in the examinations which gain them university entry and we can now proceed to ask ourselves why this is.

Social research is, then, a process of asking questions, often about linkages between concepts, and then, having established a linkage (or, of course, perhaps having discovered there is no linkage), going on to refine the questions we put to ourselves, which means re-conceptualizing our problems.

These 'problems' of research can be concerned with aspects of social behaviour which may be of a practical nature, or they may be of the type variously referred to as 'academic' or even 'pure' — in contrast to 'applied'.

In the natural sciences it is quite commonplace for researchers to engage in pure research which is concerned simply with a better understanding of nature. In chemistry, physics and the biological sciences a great deal of academic research is simply aimed at trying to find out how things work. The application of such 'pure' findings may enable man to cure diseases, fly to the planets or blow himself to pieces. To pure scientists the challenge of not knowing is paramount and they gain greatest satisfaction from increasing their knowledge in an area of enquiry where many questions remain unanswered. When we read each year of the scientists who are awarded Nobel prizes in various scientific disciplines we, as laymen, rarely understand what their work is really about. Yet they are truly 'pushing back the frontiers of knowledge'. For the pure scientist, knowledge itself is sufficient goal. If there is a practical application to which that knowledge can be put then that is all to the good, but it is the applied scientist who will take over for that task. The more applied scientists, and I would argue that most sociologists are applied scientists at heart, would tend to see their research as being in a practical context from the outset. Most sociologists have some view of the social context within which they work and have views, either implicit or explicit, about the relevance of their research to the area in which they work. Even the most abstract sociological theorists usually have some 'world view' within which they theorize. The absence of theorists holding fascist views, as compared to the numerous theorists who hold communist views today, is in itself an indicator of the socially acceptable and unacceptable contexts in which people work.

Social research is normally about 'problems' — which are themselves socially defined. For a topic to become a 'problem' for research does not necessarily mean that it is a 'social problem', such as unemployment, football hooliganism or the rising divorce rate. A serious sociological study of what remains of the aristocracy in Britain today could well be designed with a view to a greater understanding of their sources of wealth and power, their way of life and the ways in which they cope with social change. The research need not be providing ammunition for pressure groups for the abolition of the aristocracy or for its preservation. But let us be realistic and accept that a neutral stance on a study of the aristocracy would be rather difficult to achieve and some social researchers would probably not want to have one anyway.

It is easier for researchers to become involved in applied research where there is agreement on what we call social problems. As national interests change, so do research interests. We have seen periods when juvenile delinquency was a popular field of study. Social aspects of education, problems of old age, race relations, sexual discrimination, and now unemployment, have all been accepted as areas where useful research can be carried out, not only to try to find out how people behave and why, but also to provide society (often government bodies) with information which can be used in the formulation of social policy. Behind this research, then, is a desire to know more, so as to be able to influence social change. The researcher may well not be directly involved in the formulation of the social policy which is decided upon as a result of his (or her) work, but the information is gathered with a clear view to making it available for policy-makers.

Not all research, of course, is necessarily going to influence the major political parties in drafting their election platforms, though some researchers do act quite openly as advisers in this way. A lot of social research is at rather more mundane levels, where questions from practitioners of the type 'Would we be better advised to do *A* or to do *B* in aiming for our goal *C*?' can perhaps be answered by social researchers. So long as the social researcher concerned is not fundamentally opposed to the goal itself or one of the alternatives to that goal then there should be no great problem in conducting research which is objective and reasonably impartial. For example, in my own researches into theatre audiences and into the reading of books I am, quite openly, in favour of more people going to the theatre and more people reading books. Studies I have made of theatre-goers and book readers will, I hope, have produced data which enlightened theatre administrators, book publishers, booksellers and librarians can use in their work. I myself have, from time to time, made recommendations about action that might be taken by them. In these research activities I have, in effect, said to the would-be policy-makers, 'Tell me what ends you want to achieve and I will try to help you achieve them.' However, if my main aim in life were to be to overthrow our current democratically elected form of government with a view to replacing it by an authoritarian form of dictatorship then it would be deceitful of me to go, shall we say, to a government-financed research council and ask them for the money to conduct research into the weaknesses in the workings of our democracy without mentioning what the ultimate purpose of the research really was.

Personal involvement in social research is extremely difficult to eradicate simply because social researchers so often choose their areas of study for their personal satisfaction. A researcher who had no interest whatsoever in our educational system would be highly unlikely to research into it; a researcher who, as a person, strongly wanted to change the system, would be drawn to researching into it. Chemists do not seem to generate the same personal involvement with their structures. A social researcher who, as a person, feels that police forces are corrupt would hardly be expected to carry out an impartial study of the police. It would be surprising if study of the role of pressure groups in modern society carried out by a leading member of the campaign for nuclear disarmament turned out to be completely objective about that body.

Social research is, therefore, a difficult field for the practitioner who is striving for an honest and unbiased appraisal of his or her chosen problem. We are all of us, even sociologists, human beings with personal feelings and our own beliefs. The problem for sociologists is that they have to work with data that stir their consciences directly. The physicist who works on nuclear power or rocket research can often separate his research work *per se* from its uses and thereby become detached from a feeling of responsibility in the applications of the work. For a social research worker this separation is not as easy to achieve since the phenomena of the study are themselves human beings. The danger is, of course, that the social researcher can so easily become personally over-involved with the research that he ends up as a protagonist for a value judgement or ideological position and in so doing forfeits his position as a social scientist. It is one thing to declare one's interest and to be aware of the dangers of partisanship, but it is another to declare one's biases and then to do nothing to try to get rid of them. Even worse is so to design and execute the research that only the evidence one wants for one's chosen viewpoint is examined and any contrary evidence is ignored.

In the discussion so far the reader will have noticed that the words 'science' and 'scientist' have been used quite a lot. It is important to understand what is meant by these words and to be quite clear about what scientific method involves. In the next chapter, therefore, we shall look in detail at the concept of science and then move on to consider the application of scientific method to the study of social phenomena.

2

Scientific Method
and Social Research

Even today, when the media of communication are forever
telling us that we are living in a technological revolution, there
is still, for many people, something of an aura of mystery
surrounding the idea of 'science'. Perhaps encouraged by
comic strips, film and television portrayals of scientists, and
especially by the multi-million dollar science fiction film
sagas, we tend to consider scientists and science as things
apart from the ordinary run of daily life. At a time when
mankind is faced with tremendous problems of over-popula-
tion and deprivation in under-developed countries we look to
scientists for the answer. In overcoming the major diseases of
mankind we hope for scientific breakthroughs. When astro-
nauts go further into space or even greater weapons
of destruction are invented it is the scientists who are
responsible.

Not surprisingly, many people's conceptions of science and
scientists are bound up with people in white coats looking
down microscopes or rows of people in front of visual display
units pressing vast arrays of buttons. If many laymen feel
that scientists are almost a race apart this cannot be surprising.
Yet science and scientific method are all around us and it is
our concern in this chapter to understand two fundamental
points about the concept of science itself. Firstly, science is
often better defined and better understood if it is considered

in terms of method rather than subject matter. Secondly, science is very often a matter of degree rather than an absolute 'is scientific' or 'is not scientific'.

Let us consider the first point of science, method and subject matter. It is not difficult to show that trying to define science by subject matter soon becomes a difficult matter when we start considering examples. Perhaps we have no problem accepting that chemistry and physics, mathematics and biology are 'sciences' since they were classified as such when we studied them at school. But are the subject matters *themselves* what make these subjects sciences? In zoology we can study horses, in anatomy we can study the human body. Stubbs painted horses and Rubens painted nude figures. Were Stubbs and Rubens scientists? Of course not — they were artists. Some people who study literature make very complicated analyses of the words used in authors' writings to study their style and sometimes to try to determine a doubtful or disputed authorship. Are the people who do this work arts scholars or are they scientists? They are probably both.

The last twenty or thirty years have seen a tremendous growth in the 'social sciences'. These developing disciplines have focused their attention on various aspects of humanity and its behaviour. Economics has even been called 'the dreary science'. Sociology, psychology, anthropology are all words ending in 'ology' which, of course, means 'the science of . . .'. But geography is a subject which may be studied academically in faculties of arts, social science or even pure science at university, so what sort of a subject is it? History is usually considered to be an arts subject (or a humanity) but some methodologists would consider that it is more rigorous in its scientific approach than are some of the subjects referred to disparagingly as the 'soft' social sciences.

So, if we try to label subjects as sciences simply according to their subject matter we quickly find things becoming difficult. It is better to adopt a different approach and to look at the *way* in which the subjects are studied. If we can agree that a certain *method* is indicative of science then we can decide that some approaches to a given topic are scientific and some are not and we can probably agree that some are *more* scientific than others because of the sophistication of the method that is used. Charles Dickens wrote some brilliant novels about nineteenth-century London. Arnold Bennett's novels of the Potteries make the life there of his day live for the reader, but both men were novelists, not scientists. Booth and Rowntree's volumes were much less readable, but they were more scientific.

But let us be clear that the two criteria I have just dealt with do not do away completely with the problems of nomenclature, since there can be various people working in a certain field using different methods. A traveller might write a book about his journeys, with a view to making money from it and, good though the book may be as a travel journal, it would not be a scientific analysis. A social anthropologist might go and live with a group of people for a time and try to understand, say, their systems of kinship, land tenure, inheritance and so on. If he used a scientific approach to understanding what was there he would be acting as a (social) scientist. If he went to study the people with the fixed objective of showing that they were being exploited by a harsh government then he might collect *some* data in a scientific manner but in deliberately ignoring other data which went against his prejudices he would be acting unscientifically.

All this adds up to the conclusion that it is possible to carry out scientific work in virtually any field of study so long as genuine scientific method is used. If we accept this point then there is no problem in accepting a person's claim that he is, for example, making a scientific study of religion, or of art. Shakespeare's plays or sonnets can be studied scientifically so long as scientific method is used. Equally, the novelist, the journalist, the propagandist and the political activist can all study human behaviour for their own particular purposes. But their work, for various reasons, will not be scientific.

The important thing is to be sure what one means by the scientific method, and I consider that the classic statement made by the British scientist Karl Pearson has yet to be bettered. Pearson said, 'The man who classifies facts of any kind, who sees their mutual relation and describes their sequences, is applying the scientific method and is a man of science ... When every fact ... has been examined, classified and coordinated with the rest, then the mission of science will be completed.'[1] Critics will, of course, ask what Pearson means by the word 'fact' and social scientists in particular will dispute the possibility of establishing facts in an objective way, but Pearson's emphasis on observation, classification and interpretation, all carried out openly in a systematic way is, I submit, basic to scientific evaluation. The better one does these three things the better a scientist one is. The worse one does them, or pretends to do them whilst not doing them, the less should one deserve the name scientist. It is, therefore, important to consider the three fundamental processes of observation, classification and interpretation and this we will now proceed to do.

OBSERVATION

We all of us observe, but we rarely observe systematically. In ordinary everyday social life we are constantly observing, using our senses of sight, hearing and even smell. In most mundane situations we tend to respond in very similar ways to easily recognized sounds and sights. If we are travelling on a train and we hear a voice say 'Tickets please' we are quite prepared to show our tickets to a man wearing the appropriate railway uniform. A lot of observation is so much a part of our ordinary cultural life that we are able, fortunately, to observe, classify and interpret with no effort. But suppose that we are in a foreign country with a culture very different from our own and we are taken to, say, a traditional ceremony of a religion about which we know practically nothing. Even here we might think that we would be able to observe what actions were taking place even if we found it difficult to understand them. But would we?

Even in what we might think of as the simplest social situation it is impossible to describe the *totality* of actions that take place. Let us consider as an example the highly ritualized marriage ceremony which takes place in an Anglican church. The 'order' of the service, the words to be used, the correct procedures for standing up, sitting down and kneeling to pray are all set down for the participants in the part of the Prayer Book dealing with the marriage ceremony, so the basic structure of the ceremony is already written down for the observer (or participant). But let us suppose that twenty separate observers were all asked to give a full account of everything they saw and heard at the ceremony. Would we really expect them to turn in identical accounts? The answer is obviously no. Apart from the fact that any attempt at a complete report of every aspect of the ceremony could be of enormous length, any one observer would find it impossible to see or hear everything that was happening at any given time. Even with notes in shorthand, a tape-recorder and a video-camera, no one observer could cover the behaviour of the whole of the congregation throughout the service. The *totality* of the situation would have to include not only physical descriptions of every person present and the clothes they wore, but also every movement they made or word they spoke during the service. Obviously, then, observation of a genuine *total* situation is neither feasible nor is it likely to be of much use to anyone.

The point is that we observe situations for a purpose. In the case of the ordinary participant at a wedding ceremony attention is focused primarily on the interaction between the clergyman, the bride and the groom. The dresses of the bride and her bridesmaids will probably be noted because such garments are usually specially designed for the occasion. The clothes of the groom, best man and bride's father are much less likely to attract attention, especially if they all wear formal morning dress, which is virtually a uniform. Such is the standardization of dress and ritual in a marriage ceremony that a newspaper reporter for a local paper can virtually write up the ceremony to a formula. A standard questionnaire could easily be used to release the reporter from being present at all. But for participants who are closely involved in the social and especially familial aspects of the ceremony there is much more to be seen than an outside newspaper reporter could see. The fact that two brothers sat well apart from each other in the church could give rise to speculation. The observation that some people were not at the ceremony at all could be interpreted as being very significant. The obvious prosperity of one family compared to the shabbiness of another could be quite illuminating. The fact, perhaps, that the bride was known to be pregnant by some people but not by others could colour people's observations and interpretations of the whole event.

This hypothetical example shows how we may observe along with other people but that we shall not all be seeing the same things. The point is that observation is rarely unselective. We usually go into a social situation with some prior knowledge of what we are about to see. Sometimes we have fairly certain preconceptions of what we are to see which blinker our observations. For example, an observer who feels strongly about crowd behaviour at football matches is more likely to note hooliganism than regular attenders who have become accustomed to it. We frequently see what we want to see because of our preconceptions and often we miss seeing things either because of our narrow range of observations or because we are unaware of the relevance of aspects of a social situation.

I think it is fair to say that the principal criterion guiding our observations in a social situation is that of relevance. We extract from a total situation those features which are relevant to our interest in a situation. There is a joking definition of a psychologist as a person who goes to a strip-show to observe the audience. As a sociologist interested in what might broadly be called consumer behaviour I have myself observed the behaviour of people at theatres, in houses of historic interest ('stately homes'), in bookshops and libraries and, most recently, in the British Museum. In all these instances I have carried out preparatory obser-vations to help me design further research work. But I recognize that simply mingling with the crowd at a theatre or museum has grave limitations. I can *see* what people are doing and perhaps, by a gentle process of eavesdropping, I might hear what some people say to each other. But I could certainly not observe the totality of behaviour of over a thousand people an hour passing through the main entrance to the British Museum on a busy summer's day. What I probably would start noticing in what I might think of initially as 'unstructured' observation would be indications of visitors being from foreign countries and the general age of the visitors. If anyone were to ask me whether there seemed to be significant numbers of bald men, or women wearing glasses, I would certainly not be able to give an answer.

Many experiments in observation show how selective we are in our ordinary observation and how often we see what we want to see. An optimistic theatre director will see an auditorium that is half full; a critic will see one that is half empty. At a conference I attended not very long ago a very talented amateur magician gave a performance to colleagues in the lounge of a hotel. We all sat around within a few feet and yet, with his sleight of hand, he was able to baffle and amaze us. Our observation must have been faulty yet we were being encouraged to observe with great care. It is said that the onlooker sees most of the game, yet at major tennis tournaments the officials are often abused for their lack of skill by participants whose observations must be partial.

The social scientist is involved in working from early crude observation towards more systematic observation and it is therefore most important that we try to see things that are there and not to see things that are not there. The problem is that social situations are so complex that we are always in danger of leaving out important factors which are of unsuspected relevance whilst giving too much attention to factors which we have decided beforehand are relevant. It would be foolish to pay a great deal of attention to factors which we decide a priori are not likely to be of relevance in our study but such a decision is made on the grounds of supposed relevance and could be wrong. To take a simple hypothetical example: if we were observing the behaviour of young people at a disco we would certainly note their sex and their apparent age. We would possibly note the colour of their skin, but we would be unlikely to note the colour of their eyes. We might observe the colour of their hair, especially if it did not seem to be as nature had intended. Why then do we observe skin colour but not eye colour? The answer is plainly because skin colour might help us to understand social interaction processes, but we do not think eye colour will. Our selectivity of observation will be in accordance with what we think is relevant to our interests. What does not seem relevant does not justify observing. Yet, let us speculate that a young man who does not seem, on the face of it (an interesting expression), to be in any way different from the other young men may be the centre of attention of a seemingly admiring group. We can *see* no reason for his popularity, but if we go further than just watching and discover that he won a huge prize on the football pools last week then we shall have new data to help us further our understanding. Observation does not stop at just watching, as later discussion will make clear, but whatever the level of observation which may take place there is a further problem for the observer of communicating his observations to other people. This leads us on to the second stage which is classification.

CLASSIFICATION

Classification is essentially putting things together which have certain similarities so that we can deal with them more easily. Very often the process of 'dealing with' them is bound up with our wish to communicate our observations to other people.

Young children learn very early in their lives to classify what they see and communicate their observations to other people. Often some of the first words children speak are of a classificatory type. 'Moo-cow', 'pussy', 'hot', 'big' and similar such simple words are classificatory words. Often a child may classify wrongly — perhaps including horses with cows, in which case he or she will be corrected. It is not uncommon for a very small child to say 'Daddy' when looking at a male who is not his or her father. Here the child has observed the general male characteristics but has applied a very specific classification rather than the more appropriate general one. The very old parlour game of 'Animal, Vegetable, Mineral' is another example of classification in which the participants gradually classify the unknown object into smaller and smaller categories using a simple yes–no response to their suggestions.

The process of classification is a way of grouping together objects, actions, attitudes, beliefs, characteristics — all sorts of phenomena which are needed to be collected together to help us understand a complex situation. In a football crowd we could classify people present as men/women, men/boys, home supporters/away supporters, season ticket holders/pay-as-you-enter spectators, football hooligans/normal supporters and so on. Classification helps us to make sense of the whole scene by putting together many similar types of people into categories which we hope will help us understand better the social aspects of the situation.

A very simple example of classification is to be found in the statistical classification so often explained in the first chapter of a textbook on elementary statistics. To describe one person according to his sex, age, height and weight is not too difficult; to describe these four characteristics for hundreds of people individually would be tedious and not helpful in describing the *general* characteristics of a group. The listener or reader who had to endure the individual details of, say, a hundred people given one by one would end up quite bewildered. So to convey to our reader a general description of the group we classify our hundred subjects according to certain useful characteristics. Sex is the simplest since everyone is either male or female and we need only two categories. For age we must create some useful *ad hoc* groups, perhaps a simple one of under-18 and 18-and-over or perhaps ten-year groups such as 20 to 29, 30 to 39, and so on. Whatever sort of classification we use (and we would categorize height and weight in similar ways), we end up by putting the people we are describing into bundles so that we can get a better picture of the group as a group.

Some characteristics, such as sex and age, are not very difficult to handle, but others present greater difficulties. A characteristic such as sex is 'discrete' since everyone is a man or a woman and (with very rare exceptions) people are not half-way between the two. The variable of age is a 'continuous' one since the graduations for measuring it are almost infinite. Even with the ages of twins, one must have been born before the other one, so if we must decide which is the older we measure age in minutes rather than years and months. But for general purposes of social analysis to classify people's ages in months, weeks, hours, minutes and seconds would be ridiculous.

Nevertheless, one can see that in classifying even relatively straightforward continuous variables such as age, height and weight, the features to be classified must be agreed on. The scales we use for measurement may differ — we might use metres rather than yards — but, on the whole, we do not have much difficulty in agreeing about *what* we are measuring. When it comes to classifying social factors themselves the problems are much greater. An obvious example in sociology is that of social differentiation in hierarchical fashion which we may call variously social class, social status, social grades, socio-economic grades, and so on. How can we agree what we are trying to classify and measure when the factors we are dealing with are so much more difficult to observe? Perhaps it is wise to remind ourselves that although we may be completely accustomed to measuring physical objects such as planks of wood or electrical flex in centimetres or feet and inches there is nothing mystical or God-given about these units of measurement. We can use and respond to the concept of 'length' in a particular way because we have agreed what the units of measurement are and we all agree to use the same measuring tools. So if I buy a yard of wooden shelving at a local shop it will still be a yard long when I get it home because the shopkeeper and I have used the same measure of length. Whether we measure the wood in metres or yards is purely a cultural action which is irrelevant to the concept of measurement itself.[2]

Agreement is not as easy when we are dealing with sociological phenomena. So often we find ourselves trying to classify behaviour associated with such vague concepts as freedom of speech, educational opportunity or bureaucratic organization. To classify the social structure and interaction which exemplifies a 'democratic society' is not easy. To find characteristics on which we all agree for purposes of classification can be very difficult. For some people a 'terrorist' may be a freedom fighter. We may have very different perspectives on a group which one person may view as a protest movement and another as a subversive movement. Social research is full of semantic traps and the answer is not simply to quantify everything and try to turn it into numbers. In the process of trying to measure phenomena by means of over-elaborate measuring indices we can be in danger of losing sight of the deeper aspects of a problem. We may measure everything but understand little. Critics of classification and measurement can be justified when it seems that highly complex measuring devices appear to become ends

in themselves rather than means to the end of better understanding. And true understanding is the concern of our third
factor, which is generalization.

GENERALIZATION

In ordinary, everyday conversation one frequently hears
people say things like 'But, of course, it is very hard to
generalize.' Indeed it is, particularly about social behaviour.
But the social sciences are all concerned with attempts to
generalize scientifically about aspects of social behaviour.

Let us suppose that we are interested in the problems
of juvenile delinquency. As scientists we want to try to link
delinquency with other observable factors so that we can
understand better the background and (sticking our necks
out) the 'causes' of delinquency. What use may be made of
our findings we will, at this stage, leave to one side. The
work we shall attempt in this field of enquiry will be that of
finding what other traceable factors go along with this
behaviour which we have classified as delinquency. If we
take one particular case of a boy — let us call him Kevin —
we may find that certain features in his background and
history seem, on the face of things, to have some link with
his appearance in the juvenile court and subsequent con-
viction. His father died when Kevin was a baby. His mother
has had a series of 'lodgers' ever since then. Kevin's elder
brother graduated from approved school, via Borstal, to
prison. Kevin's home is a two-roomed apartment with no
separate kitchen or bathroom, in the heart of a slum district.
Kevin himself is below average intelligence (though no
moron) and has a record of truancy from the local comprehensive school which he attends. A description such as this,
which is entirely fictitious, probably has us nodding our
heads and saying mentally, 'Yes, that's just what you would
expect'. Why do we accept this sort of evidence as being
something that satisfies us in our need for explanation?

If we had been told that Kevin was dark-haired, blue-eyed, right-handed and blood group O we would have been puzzled as to the relevance of this list of factors. The essential point here is that Kevin's background fits in with what has already been established about delinquents: Kevin is a particular case who fits in with the generalizations already made from previous studies. And the generalizations already made are, of course, derived from dozens, hundreds or thousands of studies of people like him.

Perhaps this all sounds rather too easy, and Kevin's deplorable social background makes him sound like a boy doomed to delinquency by his environmental factors. But to complicate the issue we find that there are hundreds of boys with similar features to Kevin's who have never been delinquent in their lives; fine, upstanding boys from broken families, living in deplorable slum houses, helping their mothers and being a joy to everyone. On the other hand, right after Kevin's case has been dealt with, we have an almost identical offence committed by Giles, the carefully brought-up son of a professional couple, educated at a private school, living in a lovely house in a select suburb with no 'problems' one could think of. Where does Giles fit into our generalization?

This is where we find ourselves saying that, after all, a generalization is only a generalization, and we must always expect there to be exceptions. We might even go so far as to say that it is the exceptions which prove the rule — though in this phrase the word 'prove' actually means 'test'. The important point about generalizations, especially in the social sciences, is that they are only probability statements, not statements of absolute certainty. Without going into a discussion of formal logic let us accept that if you cut off a person's head all evidence that we have ever had shows that the person will die. Cause and effect stand in a clear relationship to each other. Similarly, in physics we learn very early on that if we heat a steel ball it always expands. In chemistry we learn that sulphur trioxide passed through water always gives us sulphuric acid. We say 'always' because under the normal experimental conditions these results do always occur. But in sociology broken homes do not always produce delinquency; indeed, only a minority of broken homes, thank goodness, produce delinquents. But, looked at the other way round, quite a lot of delinquents come from broken homes. The value of this linkage is to indicate to us that if we have a delinquent we are likely to find in the background some evidence of family breakdown. We cannot always expect to be able to do anything to remedy the background, but we are, by establishing generalizations, helping ourselves to decide what to look *for* in individual cases.

In sociology we are concerned with situations in which we shall be content to say that under stipulated circumstances condition A is more likely to be linked with factor Y than with Z. It is of the nature of complex social situations that there are likely to be many more factors operating than just Y, and in this we are faced with the problems of multiple causation in social behaviour. But at this point it suffices to recognize that sociology is concerned with probabilities, not certainties. The good sociologist could well take as his motto for research the saying of Benjamin Franklin that the only certainties are death and taxes.

The fact that one cannot make definite one-hundred-per-cent claims to causal links between factors does not in any way detract from claiming scientific status for the research. Most sciences these days are more concerned with probabilities than with certainties. In some of the natural sciences the tremendous development of knowledge has frequently exposed previous errors or areas about which virtually nothing was known and, paradoxically, the greater one's knowledge increases the more one becomes aware of one's ignorance. Much of this process is to do with the refining of concepts. If you are trying to explain what happens if any observational situation you have to use some concepts to describe the phenomena under study. The more one learns the more one defines the concepts. So, put very simply, the concept of the molecule may suffice until one develops the concept of the atom; the atom will do until one moves on to the concept of the particle, and so on. One might say 'Ask a crude question and a crude concept will do for the answer you get.' But once one answer has been obtained the scientist will come back again and ask for a less crude answer because the points of detail are not satisfactory. The mother who is prepared to accept that her baby seems off-colour because it has 'a touch of wind' may eventually decide that there is more to the problem than just 'wind' and will take it to the local doctor who will give the baby a more 'scientific' examination. The checks the doctor uses, simple though they may be to a trained medical practitioner, use concepts far beyond the understanding of the lay mother.

In social research the process of coming back again and again to refine the concepts has not been developed very far, but it lies at the heart of scientific enquiry. If we say that the development of reading habits among young children depends greatly upon their home backgrounds then what do we look for in the home background? We may say that middle-class home backgrounds seem more productive of book readers than do working-class ones, but then we ask what do we mean, especially in this context, by 'middle class' and 'working class'? Does the fact that one child's father is a bank manager and another child's father is a bus conductor really act directly on the child's interest in reading? Are we talking, then, of 'life-styles' associated with social class? All these sorts of questions demonstrate very clearly that continuing scientific research throws up more questions than it answers because the very fact of knowing something at the lower level of explanation stimulates the researcher to want to go on to know at a higher one. Sometimes the weary researcher feels that he is, as the student is said to have claimed to be after a difficult lecture, 'confused at a higher level', but the challenge is there.

This endless questioning of the present level of knowledge and the pursuit of more detailed understanding of what must be more limited fields of enquiry can be seen in the increasing specialization necessary in scientific enquiry if true scientific knowledge is to be gained. The day of the all-knowing 'general' scientist is long past in the physical sciences, and it is practically past in the social sciences also. Social scientists today who have not specialized in their research are likely to be generalizers at a very low level of scientific quality.

The true scientist today, as the old tag said, 'knows more and more about less and less'; only the second part that 'he eventually ends up knowing everything about nothing' is taking things just a bit too far. But to know more and more about less and less is indicative of the increase in scientific knowledge, since this demonstrates the development of knowledge from crude beginning generalizations to detailed, highly specific generalizations in carefully selected fields of enquiry. What the old tag leaves out is the tremendous growth in science and scientists over the past three centuries. Not only has there been a scientific revolution but also, to use another catch-phrase, there has been an information explosion. Information today is so widespread and is developing at such a rate that many people feel the concept of 'the library' will have to be revolutionized if researchers are to be able to gain access to the wealth of information being produced.

Science, then, is a continuous process of accumulating knowledge and as it expands it inevitably becomes more detailed. Our observations and classifications, our descriptions of social structures and social processes, will become more detailed and more sophisticated. Our generalizations from earlier somewhat crude and low-level statements applying to somewhat ill-defined concepts will become more numerous as they are more specifically related to clearly defined problem areas in sociology, and the generalizations will be more sophisticated for these reasons. The history of sociology itself clearly shows this trend, from the earlier days when sociological generalizations were pitched at the level of whole societies, to the present day where such wide but low-level generalizations are almost wholly eschewed as being too crude to be fruitful.

OPERATIONAL DEFINITIONS

In looking at work involved in observing and classifying we have seen some of the problems that are involved in trying to gain agreement on how to describe social phenomena. Suppose we want to enquire into social behaviour in a residential area and we have an idea that this is affected by the general positions people hold in society. We may phrase this sociologically by the use of shorter concepts such as 'neighbourhood interaction' being affected by 'social class'. We might even carry out research and end up with a generalization that neighbourhood interaction is conditoned by social class, but if we do this our readers will want to know what these terms mean. There are two very good reasons for this. Firstly, readers want to know in more detail just what these shorthand-type concepts mean, and secondly, they want sufficient detail to be given so that they themselves could repeat the study in just the same way if they felt it should be replicated. Standardization of concepts is a basic scientific necessity and in research it can be done by the use of the 'operational definition'.

Perhaps the best reference for social research on this topic is the writing of George Lundberg, an American sociologist who for many years wrote for sociologists on the problems of scientific methodology. Our communication of observations is made by the use of words and, as Lundberg said,

All words are symbolic designations of some behaviour phenomenon to which we respond. It is our response which gives it 'meaning'. The meaning of anything we respond to is implicit in the response and part of it. We do not respond symbolically to that which has *no* meaning to us. Meaningless things, words or symbols are contradictions in terms; the very fact that we call them meaningless proves that they have *that* meaning, i.e. we so classify them.[3]

If we are going to use words for scientific purposes we must use them carefully and specifically. The ultimate test of the value of a particular term or concept must be its usefulness for the purpose at hand, namely, the description of behaviour so objectively as to be subject to corroboration by other persons. In his textbook on methodology, *Social Research*, Lundberg gave a full argument which is reproduced almost in its entirety here.

Scientists agree to designate each degree or kind of behaviour which their instruments indicate by specific words or other symbols. These words, so defined, may then be used to build up more complicated words, the definition of which is always reducible to the readings of standardised instruments ... Such definitions are called 'operational definitions' ... (they) are merely definitions which consist as far as possible of words clearly designating performable and observable operations subject to corroboration ... Now the degree to which the above criteria can be satisfied varies according to the stage of development which a science has reached ... It is not considered, therefore, that other definitions which are only imperfectly, slightly, or not at all operational may not be valuable in the early stages of a science, and on the frontiers of well-established sciences. They may be useful as first approximations, pending more mature developments. Highly perfected operational definitions are goals to which we strive, rather than tools to be hoped for or conjured up ready made at the outset of an enquiry.

I have quoted Lundberg because he has been out of favour with some sociologists for some years because his outlook was — dreaded word — positivistic. Yet, an interest in words and their meanings has developed in recent years in the social sciences and here is Lundberg explaining how words can be used to enlighten our understanding rather than to obscure it. If we are to study concepts such as 'social class' or 'neighbourhood interaction' scientifically we must move on from the ordinary, everyday ill-defined usage of words towards some type of definition which can be used by any number of fellow researchers. For 'social class' we cannot be satisfied with descriptions which refer to social solidarity or consciousness of group membership unless these terms are further defined in a way in which they can be observed and classified. It is no use saying that 'neighbourhood interaction' refers to how people get on together, unless we know what to look for, or ask for, when this behaviour is being studied.

The operational definition is a good corrective to woolly thinking since it forces us to consider how we can convey to other researchers the full, observable meaning of what we are dealing with. If our concepts cannot be observed by others then we are well on the way to a mystical, subjective sort of study which, by its very method, cannot be scientific.

The operational definition lends itself well to quantitative, rather than qualitative description. Numbers, rather than words, are attractive to scientists since they are symbols to which we all respond in a uniform way, and numerical linkages between factors can be expressed by means of formulae and tested in accordance with recognized statistical tests. The clear-cut attractions of numerical definition have perhaps led some sociologists to an extreme position in the move towards the scientific study of society. The desire for quantification is understandable, but it can be a desire which leads the researcher to measurement for its own sake rather than towards understanding. We should always question the actual value of scales and indices for the furtherance of sociological knowledge. The researcher who becomes obsessed with problems of measurement is in danger of not being able to see the wood for the trees. This is not, in any way, to suggest that sociologists should not try to measure. Far be it from me to suggest that measurement is not one of the most valuable of sociological methods. It is merely that measurement in itself is not enough. Measurement for a purpose — a truly sociological purpose leading to generalization and theory building — is what must be stressed.

If we decide that, for a particular research project, we will classify social stratification according to a particular scale based on occupational differences then we must communicate this information clearly to other people who will read our research so that they can check on the categories we use.

The British Registrar-General, for his classification of people into classes according to their occupations, makes available a large volume which contains practically every occupation one can think of (this is the source of such exotic occupations as 'sagger makers bottom knockers', so beloved of journalists), and if we want to carry out a study of our own in which a comparison with national or regional distributions of 'social class' would be of value, not only do we have the census tables for the country and practically every town and city in it, but we also have the guide to classification of occupations which tells us what class any occupation should go into if we want to use the same method. Given these two points, the attractiveness of the Registrar-General's classification is apparent, since it has the background data we may need, and it is also revised from time to time.[4]

In this example can be seen the attraction of a form of operational definition used on a large scale in this country. This classification has its faults of arbitrariness but they are greatly outweighed by its value in enabling sociologists to communicate with each other using terms and concepts which are standard rather than personal. To say that a suburb is very 'high class' is subjective, impossible to corroborate without much more information on what the term means, and not a very scientific way of looking at things. To give the distribution according to the Registrar-General's five categories, noting the preponderance of occupied males in categories 1 and 2 is both more exact and more useful for comparison purposes. To link this with an index based on categorized answers to a questionnaire, which gives a 'measure' of neighbourhood interaction can lead further to a neat statistical test indicating whether or not the relationship between social class and neighbourhood interaction is 'significant'. This sort of research is sometimes decried by sociologists (and others) as being mechanical or meaningless, or described by any of a variety of derogatory terms. Perhaps so, when one disagrees fundamentally with the classifications used in the measure of social class and the questions asked in the index of neighbourhood interaction. But for the measurers it can always be said that they have been open to scrutiny the whole time; there is nothing mysterious or undercover about their work and anyone could go along with the same instruments and repeat the study. In effect, the argument for this type of work is that it is trying all the way to conform to principles of scientific method, low level though the concepts may be, and crude though the measures may be. If the critics of this work are to be constructive, rather than merely destructive, then it is up to them to produce something better. The pity is that some of the critics tend to be 'theorists' who have no great record of detailed empirical research of their own. The value of the operational definition is not so much — at the present stage of sociology — that it leads immediately to quantification of data, but that it helps the researchers by agreeing about the terms that are used. If the terms used are openly described without any subjectivity or mystique about them, then people can agree on definitions to be used and get on with the work more usefully. There is nothing magical at all about the operational definition, it is simply a way of stating clearly in observable terms what one is going to talk about and then sticking to those terms throughout the research. If one finds that an operational definition used by a researcher is of value then it can be adopted by other people for their research and with the use of uniform definitions science can only be increased.

THE COMPREHENSIVENESS OF SCIENTIFIC ENQUIRY

We may now clarify the position of sociology as a science from the point of view of the application of scientific methodology to the particular subject matter of social behaviour and social structure. We have made it clear that any definition of science should be in terms of method. George Lundberg said that all that the term science, as applied to a particular field, comes to mean is a field which has been studied according to certain principles, that is to say, according to scientific method. Lundberg went on to say,

If our knowledge of a certain field has been derived according to this method, and if that knowledge is applicable to this field for purposes of prediction (and perhaps control), then that body of knowledge may properly be designated as a science, regardless of the nature of the subject matter. The test of the thoroughness (or success) with which the method has been applied is found in our ability to predict the behaviour of classes of phenomena under given conditions.

Scientific method, then, is distinguished from non-scientific method in a number of ways. First of all, scientific method is distinguished by its motive, in that it aims at the discovery of truth, and truth alone. Some people may disagree with this, but it is held here that science is detached from emotional, personal, or ideological objectives. The aim of science is to attain objectivity, impartiality and unbiased observation, and if these criteria can be met then social research becomes more scientific.

Also science is distinguished by its continuity and its comprehensiveness. This means that science is not just a collection (or even a rag-bag) of individual pieces of research and empirical findings. A science is a connected framework and it is in the building-up of theory that a science reaches its maturity. Sociology, therefore, to be considered as a science, will be seen always to be seeking to establish a connected framework in which generalizations may be related. And the more these generalizations are made the more one can see the precise form which the generalizations will take. This leads to the third point, then, of exactitude. In all sciences exactitude is sought in the observations and studies carried out. The description of social phenomena is difficult enough at any time and sociology suffers particularly from the difficulties of attaining exactness in its description and measurement. But, nevertheless, this is a criterion of scientific enquiry and it is therefore a goal to be sought. It may be noted that the discovery of objective truth was particularly commented on by Sidney and Beatrice Webb who themselves were very much concerned with the developments in the methodology of the social sciences and were aware of their own extremely strong personal biases about the society in which they lived. The Webbs said,

Most people, without being aware of it, would much rather retain their own conclusions than learn anything contrary to them ... Most beginners do not realize that a good half of most reseach consists in an attempt to prove yourself wrong. It is a law of the mind that, other things being equal, whose facts which seem to bear out his own pre-conceived view of things will make a deeper impression on the student than those which seem to tell in the opposite direction.[5]

It is difficult to know on what series of findings the Webbs' 'law of the mind' was based, but there is nevertheless great wisdom in this statement. Social researchers must always try to stand neutrally at the centre of things and they, more than any other type of scientist, must be constantly aware of the dangers of seeing only those things which they want to see and not seeing those things which appear to tell against their own biases.

In the next chapter we shall look at some of the major problems with which the social researcher is faced in working towards the development of theory, bearing in mind the importance of scientific methodology in the subject.

3

Basic Steps in Social Research

SOME WRONG IDEAS ABOUT THE CONCEPT OF THEORY

The way in which the word 'theory' is used in everyday speech, and even at times by some social scientists, can lead the beginner researcher into some of the most unfortunate errors imaginable. A prevalent, though completely erroneous, idea often held by students and laymen is that theory is synonymous with speculation. The mistaken view is that theory refers to ideas which have never been tested. If theories are ever put to the test and proved right, then the theories disappear and they are replaced by facts, or perhaps even laws. This unfortunate way of thinking that theory is purely speculative leads to a division, not only between the concept of theory and fact, but also between what are called 'theorists' and what are sometimes called 'empiricists', or even simply field workers. The truth of the matter is that theory is derived from findings which are put together, and the logical relations between findings together build up theory. Looked at in this way theory then becomes the ordering of facts and findings in a meaningful way and this ordering and building up is of the very essence of scientific enquiry, since without ordering facts and without putting them into some systematic framework there can be no generalizations and no predictions. But prediction is not synonymous with theory. Theory in fact is the building which is made from the hard-won bricks of research studies.

It is sometimes useful to think of the findings of science, that is to say the meaningful observations made and their linking together, as being contributions to a kitty which is the theory of the subject. Looked at in this way one sees empirical observations, facts, research studies, and so on, as contributions to this kitty and the bigger the kitty, the greater the development of the subject itself.

When the findings have been put into the kitty then relationships between facts and relationships between research studies can be seen more clearly and these in turn will lead the knowledgeable research worker to spot the points where further enquiry needs to be made.

It is by no means uncommon for exploratory social research in an area where little work has been done to begin by looking at the characteristics of people involved. Thus, in some of my own research into theatre audiences, at a time when virtually nothing was known about who goes to the theatre, some of the first surveys I carried out were concerned with eliciting data on people's age, education, social class, who they went with, how they heard about the play, and so on. Such information was not highly 'theoretical' but it helped build up an objective picture of the people who went to the theatres I studied and gave me a useful corrective to people who made sweeping generalizations such as 'the theatre is for everyone.' It may be *for* everyone who comes to buy a ticket, but those who *do* choose to go are a small minority of the population. Once one has established a 'profile' of theatre-goers it is then an obvious next step to follow up the question 'Who?' with the question 'Why?' and the research then begins to fill in the gaps in our knowledge. Knowledge of theatre-goers also stimulates one to consider other similar types of entertainment and culture. Who goes to orchestral concerts, who goes to opera, to ballet, to the cinema? Are the people different in their social characteristics and if so why? Eventually, as the generalizations are built up (and in this field of research there is still a long way to go) a 'theory' of social aspects of theatre can be built which will be based on social empirical foundations rather than shaky speculation or sweeping generalizations.

So theory is extremely useful in summarizing findings, linking them together, putting forward uniformities of social behaviour and then enabling the research worker to move a step further forward with new, relevant studies which will themselves contribute directly to the furtherance of theory. This process of being stimulated by theory to carry out further research, and research contributing to the building-up of theory, is essentially what scientists call a 'feedback mechanism'. The process of scientific research is therefore a continuous one, and seen in this light sociology accumulates its findings and brings them together to build up its generalizations and, if possible, laws of social behaviour. Pointing to gaps in our knowledge, which itself comes from adequate understanding of sociological theory, is one of the most important parts of social research and brings out clearly the importance of the research worker having a good background of theory.

This is not to say that some good pieces of research do not emerge from almost accidental findings of research workers. The whole history of science is full of examples of scientists happening to notice something almost by accident and being stimulated to ask why this has happened.[1] Why, for example, did apples fall from trees? Why did the kettle lid jump up and down? In more recent years, the example of Fleming's discovery of penicillin is a good case of the almost accidental research which was of tremendous value. In social research, perhaps the most famous example is that of Elton Mayo's study of American girls in a factory,[2] where his observations of the importance of the creation of social groups led to the development of a whole school of thought in social psychology. New facts found by accident may be the starting point for new theories and social observers are certainly not lacking in opportunities for chance stimulation in their ordinary everyday life, since they themselves live among the phenomena which they study. The difference of approach illustrated here between the apparently hard-working development from carefully formulated theory towards new ideas to be tested where there are gaps in the subject on the one hand and this last-mentioned almost accidental following-up of ideas that just seem to occur out of the blue, would, on the face of things, seem to make it difficult to use two such disparate methods of enquiry in one discipline. But it is by no means difficult if one has a procedure for social research and this procedure we shall now consider by working from an empirical approach to enquiry.

SOME WRONG IDEAS ABOUT THE WORD 'EMPIRICAL'

The *Shorter Oxford Dictionary* says that the word 'empiric' means 'based on observation or experiment, not theory'. In general, empiricism is based on direct experience only and ignores statements based on anything other than experience. In its extreme form, therefore, empiricism limits itself to the results of direct observation and virtually denies the value of theory since this is generalization removed from first-hand observation.

However, there is an important difference between what might be called the doctrine of empiricism, and scientific theory, which must be empirical in the sense that statements can be deduced from theory which are about particular events and which can be checked by observation. As Gellner has pointed out,[3] 'empiricism', as a theory of scienficic method and knowledge generally, can mean two quite different things. On the one hand it can be used simply to say that whilst theory is essential and desirable it nevertheless depends for its validity on observation (of an empirical kind). This view of 'empiricism' would be upheld by a substantial proportion of scientific workers. On the other hand, 'empiricism' can be an extreme viewpoint which denies the possibility of theorizing and can even hold that theory is undesirable. Such a viewpoint is not generally subscribed to but can be felt to be, in certain instances, a useful counter-argument to flimsily-based 'theorizing' where the theory is really only speculation. Empiricism which, as a system, rejects all a priori knowledge and which rests solely on experience and induction is quite different from empirical knowledge gained from experience.

Data and information gained from empirical observation and experience are necessary for explanations which can then be used for the building-up of theory. The important thing is that the empirical data and the theorizing are connected, not separate, things. Sociology, as a social science, is more than just a collection of empirical findings and is also more than just a set of speculative armchair 'theories'. The empirical basis of theory is fundamental to its reliability and its validity and, in the end, its credibility, as Shipman has pointed out.[4] But the word 'empirical' is frequently used in a disparaging way by some people. Why should this be so? Why does theorizing seem to be so much more prestigious than empirical research?

Let us look at the empirical approach in a concrete instance. Most housewives and many motorists are empiricists. The housewife who knows that when her electric iron ceases to work she must replace the fuse (let us say it is a cartridge fuse in a 13-amp plug) is an empiricist. She observes that by taking out the old fuse and putting a new one in she has caused the iron to work again. Similarly, the motorist who discovers that he should pull out the choke button a particular amount so as to get the car to start on a cold morning is also an empiricist. He notes that too little choke does not work, yet too much choke does not help either. Just why the particular setting should be effective does not worry the motorist particularly, since he is only concerned with one car, not motor engineering in general. The practical empiricist is the person who knows where to slap the television set to cure it of flicker, the little dodge that stops the Yorkshire pudding from being flat, the combination of household ingredients (a teaspoonful of salt, a teaspoonful of baking powder in a pint of boiling water in an aluminium container) which cleans the tarnish off silver. People who have a 'knack' for things are often empircists, as are people who do things that Granny did because they work. The domestic empiricist is not concerned with the generalities or principles underlying the cooker or the car; he or she sees what has to be done to achieve a desired end and that is that.

At work there is a great deal of empiricism – sometimes it becomes almost a mystique, as in the steel-making process where the head melter was once supposed to be able to tell whether the melt was 'done' by spitting into it. A good example of empiricism can be seen in the making of magnets. I once saw a woman whose job it was to make small bar magnets from steel blanks about two inches long. On her right hand she had a large pile of blanks. In front of her she had a large electric coil, suitably insulated, and a button. On her left she had a pile of magnets which she had produced by putting the blanks inside the coil and pressing the button. Since the whole process took only a few seconds for each blank and the woman was working full-time it could not be denied that this woman knew, from her own sensory experience, a great deal about the making of magnets. Probably few people in the country could have more direct experience than she had. But her knowledge of magnet-making contained no scraps of theoretical magnetism. She knew nothing about field forces or induction or anything of that sort. She only knew how to make magnets.

Much practical work in agriculture is of an empirical type and the 'practical' farmer is often characterized by an empirical approach as contrasted with perhaps the more theoretically-based approach of his son who has attended agricultural college or university and who understands some of the theory underlying a more scientific approach to agriculture.

All sciences – physics, agriculture, medicine and even sociology – go beyond the mere solution of immediate problems, whether these problems are of a 'pure' intellectual type, or an 'applied' practical sort. But it is commonplace for studies to begin with largely practical or unsophisticated problems. From the empirical studies work then goes further and more precise definitions, control of observations and measurement of variables are introduced to add precision to the studies. From these studies, preferably repeated time and time again, we then put results together and look for links between findings and for broader generalizations. In effect, it is as if the woman making the bar magnets suddenly realized that there were more questions to be asked about her job; that pressing the button was not really much of an answer to the question 'How do you make magnets?' From the generalizations, theory is then built up, tentatively at first, and perhaps very low-level and crude, but always referable back to the original scientific observations.

In this way theory encompasses at once both the broad generalizations which lead the researcher on to further enquiries and the precise statements of interrelationships which help tidy up some of the loose ends of understanding. In the continuous process thus engendered one sees how true theory stimulates ideas about what may be, in realms as yet unexplored. The ideas which come from a good theoretical understanding form hypotheses, and this concept is our next subject of study.

HYPOTHESES

We have seen that when facts are assembled together and seen in relationship to each other generalizations can be made which help to develop theories. The theory is then not merely speculation, but is a composition of interrelated facts from which new relationships may be deduced. We do not yet know if these deductions are correct since they are as yet untested. It is in putting forward new ideas, derived from theoretical bases, that the hypothesis has its function.

Usually hypotheses seek to refine theory, since the generaliz-ations already made may be relatively low-level, crude ones, and the new hypothesis seeks to produce a more sophisticated statement of relationship. Hypotheses, then, help us to refine theory by bringing more details into consideration in areas of research which may previously have only been explored in a rather sketchy way.

The Webbs defined the hypothesis as 'any tentative sup-position, by the aid of which we endeavour to explain facts by discovering their orderliness . . . Without the guidance of hypotheses we should not know what to observe, what to look for, or what experiment to make in order to discover order in routine.' Since the hypothesis is a tentative sup-position, it can normally be stated by beginning with the word 'that'. For example, a hypothesis might be 'that regular theatre-goers are middle-class in their family backgrounds'. This way of putting the hypothesis is useful in that it does two things. Firstly, it produces a flat statement of fact which can be put to the test, and, secondly, it states the case in an extreme, or 'ideal', form, eschewing such modifications as 'most', or 'a majority'. The second point will be dealt with by the research, which is likely to give an answer in percentage form anyway, so no harm is done in stating the hypothesis in the 100 per cent form.

Of course, not all social research, not even all sociological research, is based on openly stated hypotheses. Much research which contributes useful information to sociology is carried out by non-sociologists, and perhaps the best example of this is the decennial census of population without which British sociology would be hard pressed for much data about our society. The population census does not start from socio-logical theory and does not concern itself with the formulation of explicit hypotheses. It is based on the agreed belief that a regular count of several basic demographic factors is vital for an understanding of the structure of our society, and at each census it is customary to ask certain specific questions which deal with current matters of special importance.

In the past some of the most famous research studies carried out in Britain by means of social surveys have not been concerned with testing hypotheses. Neither Charles Booth nor Seebohm Rowntree were sociologists; they were just wealthy men with strong social consciences who were interested in the problems of poverty and were able enough to carry out quite sophisticated studies of this phenomenon in London and York at the end of the nineteenth century. Booth and Rowntree were more concerned with getting the measure of poverty than with trying to devise a general theory about it. Though Booth's study did produce categories of poverty which showed that many people who were in employment were still below the poverty line, and Rowntree's work was memorable, not only for the detailed way in which he examined the financial needs of households, but also for his concepts of 'primary' and 'secondary' poverty and the 'poverty cycle'. The great Merseyside Survey of the 1930s carried out from Liverpool University was mainly concerned with unemployment and poverty and, like many local social surveys carried out up and down the United Kingdom, sought to measure the incidence of certain social problems with a view to providing sound empiricial data upon which local and central social policy could be based.[5]

In general, though, the feedback to theory from many social enquiries has been almost incidental, since much research actually concerned with collecting first-hand information has been orientated to solving practical social problems, and much theoretical work has not been backed up by actual field investigations. Such has been the division that to describe a sociologist as a theorist is almost to suggest that he does not engage in field studies. This sad, artificial division between the theoretical and the empirical is quite unnecessary, but reflects the structure of the sociological profession itself, affected as it is by its history and its own peculiar form of development in Britain.

True sociology is never divorced from theory, yet it never builds its theory without facts, and the hypothesis, I contend, is the crucial link between the two. Background knowledge derived from population censuses, market research surveys, government annual abstracts of statistics, historical records and so on, are all grist to the mill of the social researcher. But when scientific method is employed to keep the work of sociology along the lines of a growing discipline then a close relationship between theory, hypothesis and facts must be maintained.

The problem of designing a complete research project is frequently encountered by university lecturers who have to supervise undergraduate dissertations which are supposed to have some element, no matter how small, of 'research' in them. Students frequently come to their supervisors and tell them that they are 'interested' in old people, television, advertising, or some such huge idea. There is nothing wrong with being interested in, say, television but that does not make them research social scientists. On the other hand, the student may say that he or she is interested in Marx's concept of alienation or Weber's concept of bureaucracy. Here one immediately has a sociological concept to work on – but to what purpose? Does the student follow the old adage that to read and paraphrase one book is plagiarism but to use two is research? Just what is the student going to *investigate*? The best undergraduate studies usually come from the students who can see the possible application of a theory or concept to a specific empirical example. Thus I have seen an interesting application of group dynamics to the study of a Women's Institute, and a voluntary social agency studied as an example of a bureaucracy.

The importance of focusing on a manageable instance was well brought out in an American textbook on statistics written many years ago. Its author, Margaret Hagood,[6] wrote:

Students who are inexperienced in research frequently fail to narrow and focus their efforts to achievable units. When thesis subjects as broad as juvenile delinquency in the South or differential fertility in the U.S.A. are chosen — subjects which transcend any bounds of accomplishment during graduate work and which are not definitely formulated – they are likely to bring the young research person to a state of despair when he realizes that the masses of material he has assembled answer no questions, neither confirm nor refute any hypothesis, and yield nothing toward developing a scientific sociology. The beginning social research worker can make most certain the value of his contribution if he narrows his research to very specific problems. By these bits scientific knowledge grows, and by revealing these bits the student learns not only the importance and full meaning of knowledge itself, but also the valid methods of acquiring knowledge. Thus he trains himself eventually to tackle larger problems and to gain insight into the underlying principles by which these limits may be synthesized.

These words of wisdom remind me of a student who came to see me many years ago after the long vacation during which she had begun her undergraduate dissertation (with another tutor who had left the university that summer, I must emphasize). Her supposed research topic was 'Interpersonal relationships and group structures in a student farm camp'. The poor girl had gone off to her camp before she had formulated any hypotheses; she had no idea as to what theory or concepts her work was to throw new light on, and so, to be on the safe side, she had recorded everything she could think of over a period of about six weeks and her notebooks practically filled a medium-sized suitcase. With this rubbish tip of information she then came to me to ask how she could write it up into a dissertation.

Although this was an extreme case, it is by no means unique and practically every university teacher who has supervised an undergraduate dissertation will recognize the problem of trying to write a dissertation backwards; that is to say, taking the data that have already been collected and then trying to find some hypothesis which they can be used to test. It is very difficult to do this satisfactorily; the experienced reader can nearly always see where the joins have been made and, of course, for the student the exercise in beginning research has been carried out the wrong way round. It is all rather like the trial in *Alice in Wonderland* – sentence first, verdict afterwards.

Let us accept that by no means all research stems from the

reading of published theoretical work or dissatisfaction with the use of concepts. Much useful research can originate from the idea that just turns up, the hunch or the observation of something that happens in the street which triggers off a line of thought. The study of society would be a chair-bound discipline indeed if its practitioners did not move about in society looking for ideas. So sociologists can be stimulated by everyday occurrences which they, because of their training, can see from a special perspective and which they can put into a sociological frame of reference. Whatever may be the instigating factor in a piece of research, whether it be a random observation or a sudden thought in the library, there is a common form of procedure which can be used for the research.

RESEARCH PROCEDURE

Although a common form of procedure for research is being recommended here it should not be thought for one moment that a hard and fast programme is being suggested to which every research enquiry should conform. Social research is happily so varied in its subjects of study that a wide variety of techniques may be used for many research projects. For ease of reference, the various steps are numbered, but the divisions between the steps should never be thought of as hard and fast. In some research projects carried out mainly in the library, using only documentary sources, there will obviously be no recourse to the use of survey techniques for collecting data. On the other hand, some social survey projects do not necessarily require a great deal of theoretical background reading and the emphasis in this case will be less on the library and more on fieldwork. What follows, therefore, is an outline which is very general indeed and in no way a blueprint to be slavishly followed in every instance.

Step 1: the initial research idea

This is the very first idea which suggests the beginning of a new research project in the person concerned. A person's previous research experience will obviously determine the level of research which is to be begun. For a university undergraduate the research may be a dissertation, which is the student's first attempt at a piece of individual research. But even here the student has some background of experience to draw upon since every essay written is, to some extent, a research project. For the experienced researcher a new project may well be the extension of past research, taking problems further and trying to develop current knowledge to a higher level. But whatever the starting point may be, the researcher must be stimulated to want to pursue the investigation in the first place.

Ideas which can be developed into research projects can come to people at all times of the day or night and under all sorts of circumstances. These ideas are the 'triggers' which set off new lines of thought. Personally, I find that I sometimes get new ideas while I am engaged in activities that have nothing to do with my research at all, such as gardening, painting in the house, or even shaving when I get up in the morning. It seems that my mind is then not working at any high pressure intellectually and, somehow or other, it is receptive to completely new ideas. Simply walking down the street can trigger off ideas about society. Observing people's behaviour in department stores, in hospital waiting rooms, in the theatre, or on a camp site can all, in various ways, result in ideas about patterns of social behaviour. Also, listening to people's conversations can be very enlightening and suggestive of ideas. Recently, my wife was on a local bus with a lot of teenage girls coming home from school. One girl asked another if she had had a lesson on computers that afternoon and when her friend replied in the affirmative her short comment was 'Dead boring, isn't it?' So much for the younger generation and their attitude to the new technology.

This little incident could well be the starting point for a very interesting research project.

On the other hand, social scientists can often be stimulated to develop research by a combination of not knowing enough about an area and being dissatisfied with the current state of knowledge. When I was a young postgraduate research worker my doctoral thesis began from a discussion in a staff common room on the concept of 'community'. I was myself interested in this concept but found that the word was being used by my colleagues in all sorts of different ways. From this initial dissatisfaction my own doctoral thesis developed.

It is obvious from the above that researchers are drawn to research in areas which interest and stimulate them. This may seem a ridiculously simple statement to make, but awareness of our interests in research is very important. In social research we should be trying to carry out objective research to find out the truth of the matter. Therefore, we shall be attracted to areas of research which seem interesting to us. If, for example, we have no personal interest in politics or religion, then we are unlikely to want to research in these areas. Yet if we are very politically active and have strong political views there can be a danger in our working on aspects of political activity. It is more than a matter, however, of just declaring our personal commitment to one viewpoint and then hoping that this will resolve all problems. If we have hoisted our colours to the mast and deliberately ignored a lot of evidence our research, as well as our views, will be hopelessly biased. So, for the social researcher there is some danger in being too keen on the subject one is researching, but one would hardly research an area that was not of interest. My personal view is that one can be more perceptive in a project where one finds the whole field fascinating, but it is vitally important to try to find a neutral position. Although I am myself very much in favour of people going to the theatre and reading books it is very useful for my research for me to play devil's advocate on these activities and to ask 'Why should people go to the theatre?' and 'Why should people read books?' As leisure activities, both of these are minority interests in Britain – theatre-going especially so. Therefore, much as I may myself enjoy theatre-going and much as I may cheer when I see a full theatre, I must contain my own enthusiasm if I am to be a cool observer.

Step 2: relating the initial idea to current knowledge

Not every idea wae have is going to end up as a full research project. Some ideas will be too trivial, some would be impossible to carry out. But whatever our idea may be we must put it into some perspective. Thus, an idea on a social form of activity must be related to what is already known in sociology if our research is to make a genuine contribution to sociological knowledge. The initial idea must be put into a theoretical context and we must find out what work has already been done in our area of interest.

Let us illustrate this particular step by an example from life. A sociologist was present at a christening in an Anglican church one Sunday when two babies were being baptized. One set of parents were regular church-goers and genuine believers; the other parents had probably never been to church since they were married – they were merely exercising their rights, within the established Church in Britain, to have their child baptized in the parish church. The initial reaction is to wonder why two sets of parents should be undertaking an identical ritual and yet, obviously, have such different approaches to it. The hypothesis is advanced that for one set of parents the baptism is a religious ritual, whereas for the other it is a social one. From this initial thought the sociologist goes on to consider baptism as a 'rite of passage' and scans the library in both the sociology and the social anthropology sections for previous writings which will give more information about baptism in other cultures and also about the significance of rites of passage in both primitive and advanced societies. He will undoubtedly find that the very term 'baptism' is a difficult one to use all the time, since it really refers to the rite of immersing in or sprinkling with water as a sign of purification and, with Christian churches, admission to the Church. The act of giving the child a name, which accompanies the baptism, is not explicitly brought out in either the term 'baptism' or the more commonly used 'christening', since the latter, obviously, means making a Christian of the infant.

So the sociologist seeks concepts among descriptions of initiation rites in non-Christian societies and in all this learns more about the general purposes and beliefs which surround the admission of a young child into the culture into which he or she has been born. The sociologist then finds that this general picture (the theory) suggests certain ideas which may explain why non-Christians wish to have their babies undergo a ceremony in a religious belief to which they themselves do not subscribe. And he will find all sorts of possible explanations for the choice of godparents who are friends of the non-Christian couple, equally non-religious and yet quite happy to vow that they will, in the name of the child, renounce the devil and all his works, the vain pomp and glory of the world, with all covetous desires of the same, and the carnal desires of the flesh, so that they will not follow, nor be led by them. Having renounced all those on the infant's behalf, the godparents will then swear that they steadfastly believe in the creed and the Commandments. Made seriously, these are very grave undertakings, but no one present pretends for one minute that the second set of godparents are mouthing agreement to things they even understand, never mind believe. The ceremony, as a religious ceremony, is a mockery, yet as a social ceremony, with the gathering of relatives and friends, the honour of being asked to be godparents, the tea-party afterwards and the christening presents given (silver objects in particular), the whole thing has a significant place in the lives of the people concerned.

It is the task of the sociologist to understand all this, to find out what has been done already in this field, to see what light the general background of religious and familial studies can shed on this particular social act, and to formulate original ideas in a more explicitly sociological fashion. If he does this then a sociological perspective has been brought to bear on the first idea and the researcher is ready to go on to the next step, which will be one of limiting his ideas to a feasible scheme of work.

It must be stressed, though, that were it is said above that the researcher will 'scan the library' for previous writings on the area of study, this means more than a casual walk past the shelves of books which seem to be vaguely related to the topic. A genuine review of the literature on a topic should be a very systematic process and a good knowledge of bibliographical sources is vitally important for any research worker at this stage of a project. I shall be dealing more fully with the use of the library in the next chapter, but I cannot stress too strongly how important it is for all re-searchers to be knowledgeable about bibliographical sources and, sadly, how few social science undergraduates are actually taught the necessary skills.

Step 3: defining the problem and developing hypotheses

The researcher engaged in the social study of baptism may well decide at an early stage of the study that in modern British society baptism is more of a social than a religious ceremony. If he does this, then a hypothesis has been foward to be tested. The researcher's own observations, albeit as yet rather unsystematic, seem to be supported to a degree by what he reads in the relevant literature and in other pieces of published research. But at this stage the problem for research has not been defined at anything more than a very general level. To state the problem (that is to say the intellectual problem we have set for ourselves) in a way which enables us to go about finding a solution is not easy. Research can be carried out at all sorts of levels; we could restrict ourselves simply to reading everything we can find and produce a piece of work which was wholly based on documentary sources and which did not involve us in attending any baptisms or asking anyone involved any questions. On the other hand, we might so frame our problem that we felt it would be impossible to solve it unless we carried out detailed fieldwork. By defining our problem more clearly we help ourselves in deciding what we are going to do about it.

The initial hypothesis suggested above about baptism being more a social than a religious ceremony is so general and broad that it obviously cannot be tested without being broken down into its constituent parts. So, to get to grips with this problem we now have to break down our general hypothesis into a number of smaller ones which can be put to the test. We may find that some of the ideas we want to test are very difficult ones; certainly, in using this particular example of baptism, we are not taking the easiest idea ever put forward.

In the breaking-down process we find a number of ideas suggesting themselves. We suggest that baptism for non-believers enables a family reunion to take place. We suggest that it enables the parents to pay a compliment to close friends by inviting them to be godparents. We suggest that the choosing of the names for the child enables the parents to pay compliments to other relatives. We suggest that the act of baptizing the child is viewed with superstition as much as religious belief; that it is 'better' for the child to be baptized in case anything happens to it. We suggest that the first-born child tends to get a bigger party and more presents than subsequent children. We suggest that working-class people make rather more of a 'thing' of the whole business than do middle-class people, irrespective of their religious beliefs. And so on. With all these suggestions we are putting forward minor hypotheses which we would like to test, because added together they will give us answers to our initial broad hypothesis about baptism. It is worth noticing here that we have already begun to formulate the problem in a more practical way: that we are carving out parts of the general problem which can be observed.

Step 4: the research design

The next problem comes when we recognize that the work done so far has produced a piece of research which could easily keep a dozen people occupied for the rest of their lives. We have formulated an ideal piece of research which we could never hope to carry out with our own (almost certainly) limited money, time and personnel. So, having broken down our hypothesis into smaller testable parts we have now to decide how far we can hope to get with our present research project. One useful function of hypotheses is that they help to indicate what data are needed for their testing. The form that the argument in our research will take will show us how to use our hypotheses. Social research may well use books, journals, research reports, theses, documents, observations and surveys. It is important to consider what sort of data we shall be using and how it is to be obtained before we become over-committed to the project. In many cases the scope of a project has to be scaled down because of the restricted data available and/or the restricted resources of the research worker.

If we decide, in the case of the baptism study, that we must carry out fieldwork to collect data which is not to be found in already published sources we must consider how best to utilize what resources we have. It is almost certain that we shall not be able to mount a nationwide sample survey with sub-samples taken from the Scottish Highlands down to the West Country. We shall probably be conducting a local survey in the area where we ourselves live and work. We may decide that our· own contribution at this stage would be most usefully limited to a comparison between middle-class and working-class groups, and so we decide to do a survey in two such localities. We find it difficult to know how to obtain samples of families with recent baptisms, so we enlist the help of some local clergy who are interested, and we find that it seems simpler to restrict ourselves to baptism within the Anglican Church, since other baptisms in nonconformist churches and chapels suggest that the parents are of some definite religious following. Eventually we end up with samples of people who have had children baptized at two Anglican churches, one in a middle-class area, the other in a working-class area, over the past year. We are ready to approach these people to ask them if they will fill in questionnaires or be interviewed to help us with our research.

At this point let us take stock of the limitations we have put on our research. We have decided to study just one area, at one particular time. That is, we have chosen two parishes in our particular town — and we cannot be sure how typical the parishes or the town are of the rest of the country. This problem of the representativeness of our study can be overcome by repeating our study in other parts of the country. Perhaps in the area where we live there is a historical tradition of baptisms being great occasions, which is not the case in, say, Eastbourne or Hammersmith. In their famous study of kinship in Bethnal Green, Young and Willmott made this very point when they said, in their introduction,

The people with whom we had the intensive interviews and from whom we quote are not necessarily representative of the two districts in which they live. The two marriage samples are not only very small, but some of the people in them were more friendly, more frank and more full than others and therefore bulk larger in our account . . . If we cannot safely generalise even about the two districts we have come to know, still less, of course, can we generalise from East London to the rest of the country.[7]

Unfortunately their ideas have not been tested out a great deal in other areas of London or the rest of the country, so we cannot be at all sure whether the findings they claim are appropriate for application to the whole of our society are in fact so. But this is not to criticize Young and Willmott, since they did explicitly stipulate the limitations which should be placed on their work. If we accept the internal validity of their study we should not take the findings beyond the limits they set down themselves. So, in social surveys the limitations can be very severe, yet it would be foolish to try to avoid them. By reducing the scope of the enquiry we make more certain the worth of what we are doing (always assuming, of course, that the study itself is well conducted), and by describing carefully what we do we make it possible for other researchers to duplicate our own study or conduct a similar one with slightly different variables. The possibilities of repetition and development will depend greatly upon how carefully we conduct our own enquiry, and in particular in how we go about the next step, which is that of collecting our data.

Step 5: the collection of data

Social research encompasses such a wide range of enquiry that it is impossible to generalize about it. Even the most abstract theoretical thesis uses data of some kind, even if it is largely what other people may have said on the topic. There is a danger of thinking that 'data' must mean tables of statistics or lists of dates, but this is not so at all. Certainly, many research studies utilize historical information and the use of statistics compiled by people other than the research worker is a commonplace in social research. Data taken from the decennial census of population may well be sufficient for the purpose of a given research project on certain aspects of family structure or social class.

But other research studies may necessitate some collecting of original data by means of observation, simply because the answers to the questions being asked cannot be got except by the researcher going out and finding out. The method employed may be a postal questionnaire sent out to hundreds, or even thousands, of possible respondents — in which case the 'going out' is being done rather at one step removed —

but in this case the data are actually coming from a sample of people, even though no personal contact is made. When interview surveys are carried out, however, the researcher must actually make contact, on a face-to-face basis, with the people being studied. Not all field surveys necessitate formal interviewing; especially in community surveys there may just be one field worker living in the community. But all are concerned with observation of one sort or another, and all need to produce findings which are objective, unbiased, consistent and unambiguous. So far as possible, in the collection of all field data, the reader should be able to check the validity of reporting and should not have to trust the reporter too much.

The collection of data and the general observation stage (often referred to in general terms as 'the field work') can be an onerous step for the inexperienced researcher, particularly if the fieldwork is undertaken too soon, before ideas have been clarified or without adequate pilot studies being made to try out questionnaires or interview schedules. In general, as we shall discuss later, data should be collected because they are relevant — not just because they are interesting. If the criterion of relevance is adhered to the research worker knows why information is being collected because he knows what it will be used for. This means that a great deal of preparation needs to be made before the fieldwork begins. In the case of surveys there will always be some form of pilot survey before the researcher commits himself to the main fieldwork itself, and the more planning there is done beforehand, the less wasted time there will be in the field-work proper, and the easier will be the next stage, which is the analysis of the data collected.

Step 6: analysis of data

The methods of data collection which have been used will determine the methods of analysis. A historical study may require documentary and statistical evidence to test out a number of hypotheses. One fascinating piece of information given in E. R. Wickham's historical study of the Church in nineteenth-century Sheffield shows the pattern of pew rentals in the parish church (now the Cathedral), and the point is made very forcibly that very few seats were available for the non-renting poor.[8] In historical studies the actual quotation from the appropriate Act of Parliament or the speech from Hansard or the letter from the collected correspondence may be the vital piece of information which needs to be placed in its right position to fill in a sort of jigsaw pattern which gives what can only be the one consistent answer.

But, in the contemporary study of an institution such as a factory or a college, it may be necessary to analyse hundreds of questionnaires or interview schedules, and this will only be done successfully and without trouble if the research worker knew in advance what was wanted and how the data could be analysed before it was collected. The researcher who collects data on everything under the sun, just because it seems so easy at the time to ask a few more questions about this and that, usually rues the day when the analysis of all the answers has to be carried out. Questions which had no real purpose in the first place are unlikely to be easy to analyse at the answer stage since the researcher is seeking for answers to his hypotheses which will show whether they are to be substantiated or not.

A particularly dangerous trap in analysis has developed with the increasing use of computers in data analysis. When survey data are coded and punched for analysis by computer it is all too easy to ask the computer to carry out a range of cross-tabulations of one factor by another. This is done very quickly, but the printed results can be quite overwhelming when the sheets are received. For example, if one were carrying out a survey of library users over six days and the analysis for the working week produced, let us say, 20 print-out sheets, then to ask also for sub-analyses for each of the six days could result in a further 120 sheets. Of course, one would program the print-out so as to collate tables to save paper, but the tables of results would still have to be read and digested. If one then thinks of cross-tabulations of the users by sex, age, marital status, social class and so on, the proliferation of possible data makes the mind boggle. A good researcher knows in advance what he wants because it will be relevant to answering the problem he has set himself. There may well be follow-up questions that arise from the main analysis which can be answered by further analyses, but the attitude of mind which lies behind massive speculative cross-tabulations betrays a lack of fore-thought. The well-planned research will not present difficulties at the analysis stage, since the purpose of the answers will have been thought of in advance, and all the analysis really does is to fill in the details. These details then lead the research worker on to the next step, which is that of drawing the threads together.

Step 7: statement of results

At this stage the initially stated hypotheses will be restated against the data which have been collected to test them, and the retention or discarding of the hypothesis will take place. No sociological research is likely to produce absolutely clear-cut answers; if it were to come out with all the results 100 per cent in support of some hypothesis it would rather suggest that the hypothesis was hardly worth bothering about in the first place. In presenting a statement which attempts to generalize upon the research great care must be taken as to what is said.

Many results, especially from field surveys, may be primarily in the form of statistical tables in which percentages largely tell their own stories. But the author (and readers) will want some written commentary to accompany the figures and here caution must be exercised not to claim more than the figures warrant. Ninety-nine per cent is a majority, just as 51 per cent is, but the word 'majority' applied to both of them obscures a world of difference. The writer of the research report will want to draw together his results into a short statement of findings, which will probably be verbal rather than numerical at this stage, and where some sub-hypotheses have been substantiated and others negated the problem is not an easy one. Nevertheless, a generalization is only acceptable to the reader when it can be traced back to the evidence collected. The dubious research is that in which it is clear that the author has been disappointed not to have certain hypotheses upheld and is trying to talk (or rather write) his way round the evidence.

At this stage also it will almost certainly become apparent that a better job could have been done in the research if only more attention had been given to certain factors which had not been thought beforehand to have been of much importance. It is a complacent researcher indeed who does not look back on the research findings and wish that some things had been done better. The statement of results is the point at which these regrets can be voiced, since they can guide subsequent researchers in the field. They will also be closely linked with the final step in the research, which is that of relating the findings to established theory.

Step 8: feedback to theory

Not every piece of social research has a very strongly theoretical aspect to it and many of the more 'applied' research projects have their greatest value in clarifying limited areas of behaviour where people had not been absolutely sure what the real position was. But every piece of research carried out is a contribution to some area of knowledge and the contribution made need not necessarily be challenging the views of the founding fathers of a discipline.

When a research project is written up it will probably not be any grandiose offering (indeed it will probably be all the better for not being grandiose), but if the research has been carried out with scrupulous attention to detail and accuracy and the statement of results does not go beyond the limits justified by the data then a useful craftsmanlike job of work will have been accomplished. Most of science is built up on good solid craftsmanship and it is only rarely that the occasional blinding flash of world-shattering importance ever really occurs. It is a symptom of sociology's low status as a scientific discipline that so many researchers still seem to be seeking for the philosophers' stone, or seeking status by attempting to theorize beyond their means. Similes may be dangerous, but it can be suggested that the man who produces a well-made brick makes a better contribution to housing than does the man who builds a large mansion on insecure foundations. (This little homily seems to have an almost biblical flavour to it.) Nevertheless, a little humility does not ill become the social scientist, and a contribution to theory, no matter how small, which derives from careful enquiry, is more worthy of the accolade 'scholarship' than is the sweeping generalization based upon nothing more than armchair speculation.

SOURCES OF DATA

So far in this book we have emphasized the need for social research to be based on scientific method. This cause has been championed not because of the prestige which the word 'science' carries with it, but because it is only through the better employment of scientific method that sociology can hope to develop as a true academic discipline, free from the biases introduced by ideologists or the wish to sway current social policy.

At this stage, then, the general position has been stated as to how research workers should approach their task. The next steps will be concerned with getting down to the details of research itself, and emphasis will be placed on problems of field research. The two main sources of social data come from the inner world of the library and the outside world of living people. For ease of reference it is simpler to call these two main sources 'paper' and 'people'.

'Paper' sources provide the researcher with a wealth of information; it would be foolish to spend long hours mounting field surveys to collect information already obtainable from punished sources. Under the heading 'paper' we shall consider the uses, and some of the dangers and limitations, of documentary sources such as historical records, diaries, biographies and autobiographies. We shall also consider some of the bibliographical tools which can be used to help us gain access to published sources in the library.

When we turn later to look at 'people' as our source for data we shall consider various forms of observation (such as participant observation) but we shall be primarily concerned with the interview and the questionnaire as techniques for collection of data from this source.

Our next chapter, therefore, is concerned with paper sources.

4

Documentary Sources of Data

INTRODUCTION

For anthropological studies of primitive societies the field worker of the past often had no written sources of information to call upon at all. Primitive societies were (and a few still are) pre-literate: written information did not exist. While this obviously placed great limitations on the evidence available to social anthropologists it also spared them ·the problems of trying to find out what help they could get from documentary sources. As for the medical practitioner before the discovery of antibiotics, what did not exist did not have to be taken into account.

But most sociologists, and now many social anthropologists also, are dealing with complex literate societies in which the accumulation of documents of one sort or another has been going on for centuries. The reader who has access to the copyright libraries — which in Britain are the British Library Reference Division (better known still as the British Museum Library), the national libraries of Scotland and Wales and the university libraries of Oxford, Cambridge and Trinity College Dublin — can gain access to practically everything published in the UK since these libraries receive 'copyright' copies of all books, journals and most pamphlets and research reports. The British Library also has its own newspaper library with a vast holding both historically and in range, much of which is now in micro form. Local newspapers, of course, have their own libraries and records. Academic libraries may be expected to contain collections of research papers but too often one has to go to public libraries to find valuable collections of records and documents of local interest. With the increasing impact of information technology the problem today is sometimes that there seems to be too much information rather than too little. For social research workers to derive the maximum amount of benefit from published data they need to bring some order into their understanding of it, and for this some classification of documentary sources is needed. It is customary in research to distinguish between sources of documents by classifying them: the two terms used are 'primary' and 'secondary'.

PRIMARY AND SECONDARY SOURCES

Primary sources provide data gathered at first hand; that is to say, they are original sets of data produced by the people who collected them. They are contrasted with secondary sources, which are data got at second hand; i.e. sets of data culled from other people's original data.

The distinction between the two types is generally not too difficult to make if one knows enough about the sources of the data. In statements of a numerical type, especially, it is always sensible practice to expect the source to be given with each figure. If an author says that a third of the present holders of dukedoms in Britain have been divorced we want to know how he found this out. If he compiled this piece of information himself we have the right to know how he did it. Did he write to all the dukes and get a reply from them all? Has he talked to them and recorded their verbal yes or no? Or has he taken this statement from a book or article written by someone else? If so, who was the other writer, and where can we find where he said it, and what references did *he* give for the statement?

Obviously no one is going to want to trace every little statement back to its original source every time: life would be unbearable if we were to do this. But the whole principle is that it should be *possible* for the reader always to get back from the secondary to the primary source. It is one of the great drawbacks of much 'popular' social writing in newspapers and magazines that statements are made, the validity of which cannot be accepted without more evidence.

One difficulty of primary sources is that a purist definition tends to suggest that the writer has personally collected the information. But in much published work there is not just one writer. In the case of many British statistics of populations one can hardly say that the Registrar-General himself is the writer. He is certainly the administrative head of a large organization which is responsible for the statistics, but he does not collect data personally from even one household. But population data are regarded as primary data because the Registrar-General's department, as a single entity, collects and analyses the information. If we wish to query the validity of his data we must look at the methods employed in collecting data on various aspects of population which go into his publications. We may not always be completely happy with the published data we find in the Registrar-General's reviews but we cannot accuse him of using secondary sources when his organization has, in fact, collected all the information at first hand from the people themselves.

Another interesting problem which can arise in the publication of primary data comes from the writing up by an author of fieldwork carried out by his or her assistants. An unusual example of this occurred when I was myself collecting historical data about a small town during the course of a local social survey. I was pleased to find that a number of pamphlets on the town had been published in the late nineteenth and early twentieth centuries by a keen amateur local historian. These seemed to be excellent local background material and I was able to use quite a number of facts from the pamphlets, giving the appropriate reference in each case. But as my historical data grew I discovered, from other sources, statements which contradicted the statements of the local historian and in most cases when I checked carefully I found that he was inaccurate. One would tend to put these down to human error — annoying and misleading — in most cases; what we might call sloppy work. But in due course I discovered that the local historian had done very little actual firsthand gathering of data himself: he was a wealthy man and had employed a number of impecunious schoolteachers to be his 'research assistants'. Their pecuniary interests were probably greater than their antiquarian ones, and their errors were written up by the historian. The interesting point in this case is that the writer himself did not acknowledge the work of his assistants in his papers, so the reader had no knowledge of the writer's separation from his data.

In some modern research studies one finds that a book may be written by a well-known author, with only one name appearing on the spine and perhaps the title page. Then, perhaps in the preface, the author refers to some research assistants who have been responsible for collecting data for the study. The work itself *is* a primary source, since the data have not been taken from *other* published sources — if they are presented in a survey actually supervised by the writer. But in some instances research assistants may have been primarily concerned with digging out tables from published sources and presenting them to the writer to work on; in this case the data are certainly secondary and practically tertiary. With so much team research these days it is inevitable that directors of projects must rely on their assistants to produce satisfactory data. Then some *one* person must write up the results (even multi-author publications are not written by people playing duets on the typewriter!). It would be niggling to say that where a writer has used assistants his data cease to be primary, but it would also be foolish to ignore the fact that the more people there are involved in a project, the more opportunities there are for errors to creep in.

Another point which may be considered under the heading

of primary and secondary sources is the practice, very popular at the present moment, of giving verbatim statements made by respondents in interviews. This practice certainly dates back to Mayhew's survey of London life which contains innumerable passages of what purport to be the actual words of his subjects. Thus Mayhew, who was a journalist and not a sociologist, writes of a coster lad as saying of his life,

On a Sunday I goes out selling, and all I earns I keeps. As for going to church, why, I can't afford it, — besides to tell the truth, I don't like it well enough. Plays, too, ain't my line much; I'd sooner go to a dance — it's more livelier. The 'penny gaffs' is rather more in my style; the songs are out and out, and makes our gals laugh. The smuttier the better, I thinks; bless you! the gals likes it as much as we do.[1]

The quotations go on in this vein for pages on end for every conceivable sort of occupation. In contemporary sociology, particularly in studies of working-class life, we are often given passages which are enclosed in quotation marks. Rarely are we told how these passages, sometimes quite lengthly ones, have been gathered. If we were told that the interviewer used a tape-recorder, or that he was an expert shorthand writer, then we would know how these word-for-word quotations were made possible. But if we are not told how it was all done once again we, the readers, have a right to doubt the reliability of the evidence.

CONTEMPORARY AND RETROSPECTIVE DOCUMENTS

The distinction made so far between primary and secondary sources can be rendered even more useful if we adopt a further division of documents between what John Madge, after Gottschalk, called 'records' and 'reports'.[2] The distinction is that the record is primarily concerned with a transaction taking place *now* (e.g. Hansard, an Act of Parliament, a contract between two people, a company's balance sheet, the annual statistics for a government department), while the report is usually written *after* an event has taken place (e.g. a newspaper report, an historical account, a practical work essay). For our purposes the essential distinction is the time when the documents were written and so we will use the terms 'contemporary' and 'retrospective' to describe those documents.

With the two contrasting sets, primary and secondary, and contemporary and retrospective, we can construct a two-by-two diagram to illustrate the classifications produced, and for this four-fold classification we can give examples. Table 1 does not consist of water-tight compartments but should rather be regarded as displaying general categories which may run into each other, more as two sets of continua rather than

Table 1

	PRIMARY	SECONDARY

CONTEMPORARY	Compiled at the time by the writer
	
	Examples:
	  Court record
	  Hansard
	  Census of population
	  Newspaper report (?)
	  Contracts
	  Letters
	  Tape-recording
	  Film
	  'I am writing it now.'
		Transcribed from primary contemporary sources
		
		Examples:
		  Research report based on
		    assistants' fieldwork
		  Historical study using
		    actual documents
		  Statistical research based
		    on census data
		  Research using other
		    people's correspondence
		  'He wrote it on the spot.'

RETROSPECTIVE	Compiled after the event by the writer
	
	Examples:
	  Personal diary
	  Autobiography
	  Report on a visit to a
	    given institution
	  'I wrote it afterwards.'
		Transcribed by primary retrospective sources
		
		Examples:
		  Research using diaries or
		    autobiographies
		
		  'He wrote it afterwards.'

as two polar ideal types. Nevertheless, the four categories enable us to identify common features of some of the different types of documents which we shall now consider in detail.

Official records

These should, on the face of things, be the most reliable sources, so long as we can trust the writer. In Britain, the verbatim parliamentary record of what is said in the Lords and the Commons is possibly the most trusted document one could find. Any disagreements between members of the two Houses and the official records are carefully looked into and such is the integrity of the record that any attempt to alter it, except for errors, would undoubtedly result in a national scandal. A Member of Parliament may deeply regret what he said in the heat of a debate, but he can never have the record changed on the plea of 'I didn't mean to say that.' He can only have it corrected if the official Hansard writers can be shown to have misreported what he said. One would also tend to accept verbatim reports of judicial court proceedings, evidence given before special committees of enquiry, so long as one can genuinely believe that the people keeping the record were quite impartial and skilled in their work and that all they took down has been printed without editing. But in these cases it is necessary to know what was really going on at the time. Writing at the time of de-Stalinization in Russia, when the Twenty-second Congress of the Communist Party was in session, and Stalin's body was evicted from the Mausoleum, Isaac Deutscher used the words 'The official, *heavily edited* and misleading reports of the Congress . . .'.[3]

Of course, in Communist countries history is regularly rewritten and it is a Polish academic joke that 'only the future is certain, the past is always changing.'[4] But even in democratic societies knowledge of the past changes as historical scholarship develops and it is often found that the official record of the time under study contains errors or even deliberate falsification.[5] In the times of absolute monarchs it was a foolhardy scribe who always recorded the whole truth.

Newspapers

Newspaper reports, where a reporter was present at the scene, might be thought to be valuable, but unfortunately it has been shown only too often how little reliance can be placed on them. It is important to recognize under what pressures newspaper correspondents work: many of them do not have shorthand and use their own personal notation system. Their reporting of speeches is likely to be inaccurate in many ways, sometimes embarrassingly so. Also, a reporter can only extract a tiny part from any whole event, and in many cases he extracts what will be eye-catching and provocative. Newspapers love a good disaster, and a wedding where the bridegroom's trousers fell down at the altar would stand a far better chance of being reported than one that went without a hitch. When man bites dog it is news, but the ordinary human recipient of a canine nip would be surprised to find the national press clustered round him. It should also be remembered that newspaper people work very fast — the very latest news is always the most desirable, as is instanced by the occasional 'scoop' of the event which has not yet even happened. Reports are cut by sub-editors to fit available space, and the particular political 'angle' of the newspaper is sharpened up. In all, it is little short of a miracle that the subsequent report bears any relation to the actual occurrence at all — and sometimes it does not.

Harold Evans, once Editor of the *Sunday Times*, wrote that 'enough news is arriving today at any large newspaper office to make four or five fat novels and fill the news columns many times over.'[6] He gave as an example the *New York Times* which, he said, received over two million words a day. The raw copy which floods in from many sources is 'tasted', selected, sub-edited and, in a remarkably short space of time, some of it appears on the printed page. But Evans suggests that on some newspapers speed is valued more than polish and on a busy evening a deskman will find stories arriving faster than he can edit them.

It is not surprising, therefore, that at times newspapers publish news which is wrong. This can result in them being sued for libel; in Britain it can also result in the people concerned complaining to the Press Council, which may publicly admonish a paper for bad reporting. But speed can also result in tragic errors, as was the case in 1972 when Palestinian terrorists took nine Israelis hostage at the Olympic Games in Munich. I happened, on 6 September 1972, to be travelling to London by a very early train and bought a copy of *The Daily Telegraph* which carried the headline 'Hostages Freed in Gun Battle' and went on to say that 'late last night' there was a gun battle at a military airport in which one terrorist was killed and one policeman slightly wounded, 'but the hostages were reported safe'. When I arrived in London later in the morning a midday edition of the *Evening Standard* carried the headline: 'The Carnage at Munich — 15 die in Ambush that Failed'. This, sadly, was the truth of the matter. The nine hostages were killed by the terrorists; six terrorists and one policeman were also killed.

A further example is contained in an edition of the *Evening Standard* in 1976 where a news item reported 'at least 20 people were killed and many more feared dead or severely injured' in a train crash in Holland. Happily, this time, the late news on the back page contained a report from Dutch Railways in London to the effect that no passengers aboard the Rhine Express had been hurt. Serious errors, such as the two examples given, are usually corrected very quickly, but many newspaper readers who have personal knowledge of a news item find inaccuracies in reporting which are of less importance and which do not get corrected. Any social researcher using such reports would be transcribing inaccurate material.

But besides unintentional incorrect reporting in newspapers there is also the problem of bias, much of which may emanate from the political stance taken by a newspaper in an uncensored society. We need not concern ourselves with the views expressed in newspapers which are wholly controlled by the state in totalitarian societies. However, Stanley Baldwin, who was once the target of a harsh newspaper campaign, said of his 'press baron' opponents — 'Their methods are direct falsehood, misrepresentation, half-truths, the alteration of the speaker's meaning by putting sentences apart from the context, suppression and editorial criticism of speeches which are not reported in the paper . . . What the proprietorship of these papers is aiming at is power, but power without responsibility — the prerogative of the harlot through the ages.' (Incidentally, this reference is a secondary one, taken from Thomson's *England in the Twentieth Century*,[7] in which the actual source of Baldwin's speech is not given.)

With less serious matters the reports of social occasions can seem more like fiction that fact. Some years ago there was a wonderful letter published in the (then) *Manchester Guardian* from a person who signed himself 'Student of the Press'. He had collected together eight different newspaper reports of a highly publicized wedding between a young woman, Ira von Furstenberg, and her (then) first husband. As the bride was only sixteen and moved in 'international circles' in Italy, the press had a day-out on the wedding and 'Student of the Press' noted how the British press 'had shown its enterprise and sturdy individuality. It refuses to conform to any agreed standard even when simple facts are in question.' The various newspapers reported the bride as being anywhere between 30 and 70 minutes late: someone fell into the Grand Canal, but there were four different versions of who it was; estimates of photographers present in the church ranged from 50 to 250, and guests from 250 to 600. Of course, this particular instance was treated as a Venetian holiday by the press, and no reader of the reports would probably have cared had the whole wedding party ended up in the canal.

Official statistics

In the West we tend to trust our official government statistics and then to distrust the use made of them by politicians. But then it was a politician who coined the phrase, 'lies, damned lies and statistics', which rather blew the gaff in the first place. The census of population, the monthly and annual digests of statistics and the annual statistical reports of the various ministries and other national bodies (such as the Prison Commissioners) and local authorities produce a great deal of extremely valuable data for the sociologist to work on. We will not go into great detail on the dangers of using statistics here but merely point to some precautions which must still be taken even when using statistics which are generally regarded as reliable.

First, research workers must be absolutely sure they know what the statistics are about. In criminal statistics, for example, the definition of a 'crime' is operationally made in a number of ways. Obviously 'crimes known to the police' are greater than numbers of 'people prosecuted' which in turn are greater than numbers of 'persons found guilty'. To use criminal statistics wisely necessitates some prior work in getting to know the difference between indictable and non-indictable offences and also some legal history so that one does not suddenly discover an enormous decrease in a crime such as stealing cars when the new offence of 'take and drive away' is introduced. The various motoring offences can baffle the uninitiated, as I learned to my horror once when on a jury. Although we were trying a man for being 'drunk in charge' two people in the jury room (after a long exposition from the recorder) were quite determined to find him not guilty of 'dangerous driving' — an offence with which he had never been charged.

A popular essay topic for students is often the use of divorce statistics. Here in particular one can find an increase which merely reflects new legislation affecting causes for divorce — for example, the Matrimonial Causes Act of 1937 which introduced desertion, cruelty and incurable insanity as further grounds for divorce, adultery having previously been the only one. The extension of legal aid after the 1939–45 war was bound to affect the numbers of people able to avail themselves of this service. To ignore, or be ignorant of, these factors is to misuse statistics badly — it is no criticism of the statistics themselves.

The use of index numbers and special ratios should always be undertaken with care since they may contain hidden dangers if one does not know how they are compiled and, very often, how they are 'corrected' for a variety of reasons. It is facile to employ cost of living indices or indices of neo-natal mortality without knowing how the figures are calculated.

Not all widely used and quoted statistics come from governmental, or even quasi-governmental sources. Often we prefer our figures to come from other sources if we feel these are more likely to be unbiased. Thus, we would undoubtedly feel less happy if political polls were *not* carried out by independent agencies. We accept figures for newspaper circulations because they come from the independent Audit Bureau of Circulation. In looking at figures on television audiences we probably accept with little thought that certain programmes are frequently at the top of the list for audience rating, but we seldom ask how that audience has been measured. In the book world list of bestsellers are often challenged, usually by publishers or authors who feel they should be in the list but have been missed out because the sample of bookshops used for the research was biased against their particular type of book.

At the heart of the problem of using statistics lies the method of compilation and also the meaning of the terms used. When I carried out a survey of undergraduates and their use of books at Sheffield University I needed a sample of all undergraduates in the university during the academic year of the study.[8] It was quite a revelation, talking to the Assistant Registrar in charge of records, to discover how difficult it was to define a 'student' for my purposes. More recently I have been concerned with a survey of visitors to the British Museum, of whom there are between two and three million a year. Unfortunately, the Museum and the Reading Room of the British Library Reference Division share a common entrance, so any simple count of people walking through either of the two entrances to the building would certainly give a correct number of people *entering* the Museum, but it would not be correct for genuine *visitors* to the Museum. When one reads a figure one must always ask what the figure represents.

Diaries, memoirs and autobiographies

There may be a number of reasons for keeping a personal diary. In the case of the 'ordinary' person it may just be pleasant to record what has happened each day so that one can at some time in the future spend a nostalgic hour looking back on times past. Probably very few diaries of this sort are kept these days. In days past, when children did not have the delights of the mass media to occupy their time for them, diary keeping was regarded as a 'good thing' for the young, just as collecting things was regarded as keeping hands and minds occupied. But today the diary is regarded much more as an appointments *aide-mémoire*, and for the 'ordinary' person the keeping of a detailed diary of daily events would probably be regarded as just a little eccentric and perhaps even self-centred. Normal diaries are rare, abnormal diaries are more well-known, such as the *Diary of Anne Frank* and the *Scroll of Agony*, the diaries of a Warsaw Jew, Chaim Kaplan, who kept a diary from September 1939 until his death which was probably in 1943, the papers being found hidden in a paraffin tin after the war.[9] But even diaries of terror, such as have been published from the records of survivors or victims of totalitarian regimes, were rarely written simply for the author to look back on in years to come — for European Jews there was rarely much hope of any future. The truly personal diary, intended for purely personal perusal, is a rare thing. Much more common is the personal diary intended for public consumption at a later date. The publishing world would be badly hit if politicians did not bring forth their diaries from time to time, showing just how they reacted at the time to particular world events. And in the years after the end of the 1939–45 war there was such a spate of generals' diaries that it at times seemed difficult to understand how these men had time for the job in hand, so busy were they with their diaries.

The distinction between diaries, memoirs and autobiographies is not easy to make since one form of record can shade into the other or even contain parts of another. For our purposes, the distinction could be that a diary is written at the time of the event, memoirs are a writer's recollections of a particular period (perhaps aided by diaries) in which he was not necessarily the central character, while an autobiography is an attempt to give a systematic and chronological record of the author's life, with himself at the centre of the story. This arbitrary distinction helps us to focus attention on the importance in such documents of the contemporary recording of events. While a person engaged in a particular event can rarely see the whole set of circumstances in clear perspective he can record the minutiae of a situation which might well be lost when the position is looked back on at a later date. Published diaries which record a day-to-day chronology of events may not be the most coherent of records, but they do not suffer from being over-edited, tidied up or altered to fit into hindsight.

With politicians and military leaders the keeping of a diary is not only the gathering of data for a future book but can also be a form of self-defence in preparation for any post-mortems which might be held in the future. In a sense it is a personal keeping of the 'minutes' of what occurred at conferences or in battles which will remind the writer what happened at a precise time in the course of events. Very few 'raw' diaries are published these days unless, as in the case of wartime victims of concentration camps, they make the greatest impact by the very nature of their rawness and contemporaneity. Memoirs based on diaries, or the autobiography itself, enable the writer to make use of the diaries for the basic pattern of events, but by adding hindsight to the diaries a much fuller and perhaps more plausible or self-justifying record can be written. It is upon these sorts of documents that historians frequently draw, especially for the writing of very recent history (i.e. within the past hundred years or so) and it is commonplace to find the historian referring to 'other views' on a particular matter, as expressed by some political opponent in *his* memoirs. Thomson's brief history of twentieth-century England gives a number of examples of this sort of thing. On the issue of pre-1935 appeasement of Mussolini over Abyssinia he quotes from L. S. Amery's 'diary', which is referred to in a footnote as *My Political Life*, vol. 3 (1955) and also refers to two other accounts of the same events in Viscount Templewood's *Nine Troubled Years*, pt. 2 (1954), and Sir Anthony Eden's *Facing the Dictators* (1962). It is interesting to note in these three references the great gap between the time of the events referred to in the history, 1935, and the books referred to, their publication dates being 1954, 1955 and 1962. It is obvious that only personal documentation at the time could make it possible for these three politicians to write anything with accuracy from 20 years after the events had taken place.

One of the difficulties of using politicians' or military leaders' diaries is that they are always likely to be personal justifications of their own actions at the time, and of course they give the impression that the whole of history consists of political intrigue or war. For the sociologist who is not exclusively interested in politics or militarism some of these diaries, memoirs and autobiographies have relatively little to contribute. What personal records there may be of more general 'social life' have the limitations that their authors are rarely 'ordinary' people. Recollections of high-born people are far more common than those of the low-born. The series of books by Osbert Sitwell on his life are quite fascinating, but by no stretch of the imagination can the Sitwells be equated with 'ordinary' people – indeed, it is their eccentricities which fascinate. But the bulk of our population lives working-, or pretty humdrum, middle-class lives and the lack of documentation of these is often noticeable. Perhaps one of the best autobiographies (although written in the third person) is Flora Thompson's *Lark Rise to Candleford* (1945), followed by her later (and not, in my opinion, as good) *Still Glides the Stream* (1948). Her record of her rural childhood and young adult life in Britain at the turn of the century is a fund of sociological insights and is far more fascinating to read, and incomparably better written, than practically any genuinely sociological work of the time. But Flora Thompson was simply a gentle recorder of her own not very exciting life: the beauty of her book lies in the skill of the writing and her ability to make everyday events of interest to her reader. She was not writing of slum life so as to shock the reader, or even indulging in nostalgia so as to entertain. The simplicity of her books is above any attempts to write down to anyone.

A more recent, and very successful, memoir of childhood days in Salford was Robert Roberts' *The Classic Slum* (1971). This was written late in his life and with his own declared interest in socialism and sociology there is a tendency to see things rather more 'socially' than one might expect from a child of the local corner shop. Nevertheless, Roberts describes a way of life before and after the First World War which is quite fascinating and now, obviously, long past. His book is good reading, social history and full of sociological insights into a period which saw great social changes.

Perhaps the most deliberate use made of autobiographical sources is to be found in Thomas and Znaniecki's study of the Polish peasant in Europe and America,[10] where use is made of a specially commissioned autobiography written by a young man, Wladek Wisznienski, at the request of the authors. This life history, which extends to 311 pages, deals mainly with the writer's early life in Poland and his travels before coming to America; in fact he only goes to America 17 pages from the end, at the age of 27. But to refer to Wladek as 'a typical representative of the culturally passive mass which constitutes in every civilised society the enormous majority of the population' is to do less than justice to a tale which is at times very lively indeed and which was surely not written by any 'passive' sort of person. After all, how many educated young people of 27 could produce 300-page life histories, even today?

If we must be so very careful, then, in using what people write about themselves, would we do any better to turn to what other people have to write? Are biographical works likely to be more reliable?

Biographies

First, let us consider the basic difference of approach to autobiography and biography. In the previous section we have seen how public figures often write about themselves for a variety of reasons — one of which could just be straightforward self-centredness. But unless a person is willing to subsidize the publication of his own autobiography or memoirs, he must convince a publisher that the book will pay its way. The autobiography of a nobody must have some sales appeal. In the case of the biography the author is even less likely to be attracted to writing at second hand about a nobody, and what is more, he has a completely open field of all the somebodies that he chooses to tackle. The biographer, therefore, is likely to work on people of some fame, whatever their spheres of activity may be, and so the biography is more likely to be about the famous (or notorious) person, the outstanding success or the eye-catching, unusual personality. Controversial figures in public life, such as Winston Churchill, Richard Nixon, Indira Gandhi, Martin Luther King, T. S. Eliot and many others, will probably attract biographers for years to come because it is felt that there are still new things to be said about them, new perspectives from which their work can be seen, and new interpretations of politics or the arts in which their contributions should be judged. But even if we tend to look for the scholarly, non-involved biography of the great man or woman we cannot be sure that the work will be beyond criticism. Scholars tend to form schools of thought, and it would be naïve of the sociologist (especially the academic sociologist) to think that his history or English colleagues were blessedly free from personal bias in their views on people and their roles in the history of politics or the arts.

Many biographers fall into a category which might be described as scholarly but not academic in that they are written by professional writers for an educated general readership rather than for the narrower market of academic specialists in a particular subject. In the case of some such biographies the biographer may be concerned with the defence of a dead person, which is sometimes the case with biographies written by loving sons or daughters. In other instances the biographer may have been commissioned by the family of a person who has died to write a biography with their autorization and co-operation. This type of biography must be particularly carefully scrutinized since it may be lacking in much criticism of its subject.

My own first research experience using biographical data was when I was studying the history of housing management in Britain and, inevitably, I looked into the work and times of the great nineteenth-century housing management pioneer, Octavia Hill. She was a fascinating person. But from my own researches it became plain to me that she was very much a person of her times, as compared with Beatrice Webb who became so much a critic of her times. Octavia Hill believed, with most other Victorians, that housing should pay its way; to her, housing subsidies were unthinkable. When asked by a government committee what people were to do who could not afford 5s. a week rent for a room, her answer was, 'I should have thought that when the cost of living rose the wages must necessarily rise, or something more efficient be done. People must emigrate for instance. I should leave prices to supply and demand.'[11] She also took the view that it was not necessary to have individual access to water and drains. 'If you have water on every floor [of tenement buildings] that is sufficient for working people. It is no hardship to have to carry a pail of water along a flat surface.'[12] These quotations are not in any way intended to disparage Octavia Hill and the work she did. But the standard biography of her did,[13] in my opinion, leave out too much of the rather conservative views she held and therefore gave the impression that Octavia Hill was a rather kindlier and gentler person than she really was. The limitations of her views are just as important as her vision if the researcher is to gain a full perspective of her work and times. Charity at 4 per cent interest was nothing to be ashamed of in the nineteenth century and it was much more commonplace for unsatisfactory tenants to be evicted than is the case today. It is necessary to appreciate these facts if social policy is to be seen from a sociological perspective.

Another interesting point in biographical/historical work is the use made by later writers of their subjects' own diaries and records. In a review of two books on the 1914–18 war, written many years ago, the historian and critic A. J. P. Taylor said, 'There is one piece of advice which can be given to all generals, successful and otherwise: "Do not keep a diary" ... Though they are not much good on paper – if they were they would not be generals – they cannot resist the squat little volumes. Down each evening go the indiscretions, the jealousies, the blunders and miscalculations. Sooner or later the diaries are published, and another military reputation is destroyed.'[14] Taylor goes on to say that both Earl Haig and Sir Henry Wilson offer the same salutary warning against the publication of diaries. Wilson rose to become Chief of the Imperial General Staff at the end of the war and he was made a viscount, but with the publication of a book based on his diaries in 1927 'Wilson's reputation was blasted . . . From that moment, he appeared as a political intriguer, and an intriguer on his personal account also.' Taylor then says, 'As to Haig, in Lord Beaverbrook's classic phrase: "With the publication of his Private Papers in 1952, he committed suicide twenty-five years after his death".'

One last example may be given here to demonstrate the dangers of biographers copying each other's errors. In a delightful article on 'The Art of Biography', André Maurois once wrote,

Where can the facts be found? Partly of course in printed works, but these must be used with infinite caution and constant checking. Too many biographers copy one another. I remember, when I was writing the biography of George Sand, I read in all her biographies that her grandmother had married a certain Comte de Horne, an illegitimate son of Louis XV; that the marriage had not been consummated and that the Comte de Horne had been killed in a duel. I looked up the authentic sources; the Comte de Horne turned out *not* to be an illegitimate son of Louis XV; the marriage *had* been consummated and he had died of indigestion. When I was writing an essay on Bernard Shaw, I read in one biography that he had attended a Wesleyan school and had always been at the bottom of his form. Before printing the essay I thought it safer to send it to Shaw. He returned it with this comment: 'I have never been to a Wesleyan school nor been at the bottom of my form!'[15]

Correspondence – private and public

Although these types of data are always mentioned as sources for sociological enquiry there is really only one major piece of research which used them, this being Thomas and Znaniecki's study of the Polish peasant. Their study used letters between Poles in the USA and at home to attempt to analyse problems of the integration into American culture of people from a practically feudal home culture. In all, 754 letters were purchased for between 10 and 20 cents each and the results were analysed in 50 sets under family names.

The letters were obtained by advertising in a Polish-American magazine published in the USA. Thomas and Znaniecki's study was very carefully reviewed by Blumer in 1949 and he came out with a number of general criticisms of the research in which the authors used letters, a wide variety of documents and Wladek's autobiography as data to illustrate their theoretical propositions.[16] Our concern in this section is merely to consider what use could be made today of correspondence for sociological purposes. The publication of correspondence between famous people has been used for many years for the purposes of scholastic enquiry. From Bernard Shaw's correspondence with Mrs Patrick Campbell some light has been thrown on his personal life and general outlook. Political correspondence can be a vital source for political history, but for specifically sociological purposes there are likely to be few types of correspondence these days which would be easily available and which would be of value for social research. With the widespread use of the telephone for both business and pleasure letter-writing is in danger of becoming a lost skill and probably the only letters which are kept in the home are those between sweethearts or between members of a united family. Although, in years to come, these might prove to be of social interest, many such letters refer only to domestic and personal trivia and, having personally recently discovered a letter written to me over 30 years ago by my wife just before we were married, I would not want this to be read by anyone else at all.

But even if letters are available for research (perhaps a secret cache is discovered in an old house), they still have their limitations. Skill in letter-writing is by no means evenly distributed among the population and letter-writers cannot be said to be representative of the general population. Also, in writing of events the writer is certain to have to abbreviate any descriptions very sharply. To give a full description of even a simple evening out at the theatre could cover numerous pages, and it is unlikely that the writer has the time or wish to do this. So, letters condense events enormously, and they are also probably written from a particular angle with the recipient in mind. One can imagine a university student writing two letters – one to his parents and the other to his best friend – in which he said what the rag dance last Saturday had been like. It is very unlikely that the details would be the same for the two recipients.

Letters are often a hoped-for source of descriptions of events or of personal feelings about certain things; and one source of written information which, though not in letter form but not wholly dissimilar, can be useful for the researcher, is the description written by children or young people of events in which they have taken part, or about given social situations. A very early and most interesting use of this technique was that of Jahoda who asked young people at school to write an essay about their first day at work and what they envisaged it would be like.[17] Some of the children's expectations were so heartbreakingly wrong that it was clear that much more needed to be done to inform young people about what work is really like. In my own research into books and reading I have had classes of 15-year-olds write essays on the subject of how they would feel about working in a bookshop.[18] Many of the writers gave stereotypes of bookshops which were clearly years out of date and which they themselves knew were out of date. It was evident that for many young people the 'image' of the bookshop was old fashioned, dusty, a place for scholarly introverted people, and so on. Yet many of the children had been in bookshops and knew them not to be so. Also, when describing the work in a bookshop few of them mentioned the fact that the bookseller had to decide what books to buy for his stock and few realized how much financial expertise was needed. At the time of writing I am involved, as I mentioned, in some surveys of visitors to the British Museum and I am hoping that we shall be able to get some schools who had had organized visits to the museum, to obtain essays about the visit from the children involved. If the essays describe the exciting journey, the postcard gallery, the sandwich lunch and little else, the content analysis of such essays will be quite illuminating!

Historical documents

In a sense it is almost impossible to separate out a section on documents which can be called 'historical' since all documents are by nature historical. But conventionally historical documents refer particularly to events of the past about which the main (and probably only) source of information is documentary, the participants now being dead. Even this definition is by no means satisfactory, since there is plenty of history of the twentieth century, and people alive today who have memories dating from its beginning are contributing valuable data to the expanding field of oral history.

As Marwick has argued, 'It is only through knowledge of its history that a society can have knowledge of itself',[19] and Carr has said that 'The more sociological history becomes and the more historical sociology becomes, the better for both.'[20] Historical research is, of course, a continuous process of re-interpretation of the past. Elton claims that the 'scientific, ordered, systematic study of history only really began in the 19th century' and he particularly mentions Namier and Maitland as two historians who 'brought a scientific and intellectual approach to the study of history'.[21] Historians study social change and they focus on particular events for their data. They do not try to prove causal relationships but they do try to understand how events bring about change from one state of affairs to another. The social scientist tends to study events so as to draw conclusions of a more general and rather static kind. He is often concerned with the structure of social relationships, the principles underlying organizations and the manifestation of social institutions in general as evidence at a particular time, rather than being concerned with the flow of events which attracts the historian.

A good example of social research which is based wholly

on historical sources is the work of Ashworth on the sociology of trench warfare on the Western front during the 1914–18 war.[22] He saw the trenches as an extreme social situation in which millions of men were involved in trying to kill each other while trying to save their own lives. Ashworth's analysis uses interesting concepts drawn from sociology and psychology but his data cover everything from the official histories of the war, including divisional and battalion histories, right across to the diaries of ordinary soldiers, some of which were based on notes taken during the war but written up years later. Not surprisingly, Ashworth found more published personal accounts written by officers than by ordinary privates and some memoirs were written by poets and writers to express their horror of war. With the vast literature on this part of history that is available the social scientist has a difficult task of evaluating the information upon which he can draw.

Sources of documentary data

As must now be clear from the above descriptions of possible sources of documentary data, the social researcher has tremendous resources that he can call upon for use as primary data. But also, he has available to him all the vast resources of libraries which can provide him with books, pamphlets, research reports, theses, journals, conference reports, and so on. Many researchers fail to make the best possible use of libraries simply because they know so little about the bibliographical tools that are available to help them.

Let us begin by recognizing that the more advanced research workers are in their particular fields of research the more they are likely to want to use specialist research literature (such as journal articles and research reports) and the less, on the whole, they are likely to want to use general books. Not only do books often tend to be rather broad in their approach to a subject, but they can also take a long time to be published after they are written and the information may thus be out of date. On the other hand, although some research journals can be slow in publishing articles they are usually published quarterly, with the object of providing up-to-date findings. Research reports, which may be published in A4 format by the offset litho process, can often be available only weeks after a research project has been completed.

So, the research worker should know something about the main ways to obtain information from the library. If we are the very beginning of a project and, perhaps as an undergraduate, know very little at all about our chosen topic, we may actually start with articles from encyclopaedias. The *Encyclopaedia Brittanica* contains many useful articles on a wide range of topics and the *International Encyclopaedia of the Social Sciences* is more specialized. Unfortunately, encyclopaedias are very expensive to compile and publish so one cannot hope for a new edition every year and the information in them is thus often very dated. *The International Encyclopaedia of the Social Sciences* was last published in 1968 so, while it is useful for general articles, its facts are now very out of date indeed.

Books themselves fall into a number of categories and the beginning researcher may start from a textbook, a book which reviews a field of research or a 'reader', which brings together excerpts on a certain topic. Many such books contain useful bibliographies and advice on further reading. To find out what books have been published on topics of interest one can use the *British National Bibliography*, which since 1950 has listed every new work published in Britain, accumulating from weekly to monthly and to annual publication. The *Cumulative Book Index* is an American publication which claims to be a world list of books in the English language. Other very useful sources for the social researcher are the *London Bibliography of the Social Sciences* which is, in fact, the published catalogue of the acquisitions and holdings of the library of the London School of Economics, a major social science library; and also the *International Bibliography of the Social Sciences* which has annual volumes devoted to sociology, political science, economics and social and cultural anthropology. Both these publications cover much more than just books and the *International Bibliography* is very good for foreign-language journal literature.

There are many specialized bibliographies published on limited subject areas. For example, I have found in my own reading research that a specialist bibliography entitled *Readers and Library Users*, by Martin Ward,[23] has been very helpful in making me aware of research studies that I had not come across before. Unfortunately, *ad hoc* bibliographies date quickly and are not always brought up to date after initial publication. The *Bibliographic Index* is a good source for all sorts of bibliographies and includes many contained in books themselves.

Journal literature is very widespread indeed and any researcher may find himself having to read not only in an academic subject area but also in the professional or trade journals too. Thus, when I was an urban sociologist I read in sociology and in the professional journals of town planners. In my research into reading habits I regularly read the trade journal the *Bookseller* for publishing and bookselling news and the *Library Association Record*, published by the Library Association for its members, for news in that field. Ulrich's *International Periodicals Directory* is usually to be found in large libraries and is the recognized international list of periodicals. There are so many periodicals published that some researchers find the row upon row of them on library shelves very daunting. Fortunately, the researcher does not have to go through the bound volumes one by one to see what they contain. A journal called *Current Contents: Social and Behavioural Sciences* brings together the contents pages of the most recently published journals, but a range of indexing and abstracting journals can be used to find out about the contents of journals without having to go to the journals themselves.

Indexing journals (often simply called indexes) give the straightforward bibliographical details of articles in the range of journals (which may be in hundreds) covered by the indexing service. So the author, title of the article, name of journal, volume, number, date of publication and page numbers will all be cited. Usually an index will be arranged so that the user can search for articles by both subject and author. An abstracting journal (or abstract) differs from an indexing journal by adding to the indexing material a short summary, or abstract, of the article referred to. This additional information can be very useful indeed in saving the researcher from looking up an article which sounds as if it would be useful from the title, but which, in fact, is not relevant to one's particular interest. (In a similar way, an 'annotated' bibliography usually contains some notes on the contents of each item included.)

In social research *Sociological Abstracts* is the main abstracting journal for sociology, as *Psychological Abstracts* is for psychology. Two very important indexing journals not always used as much as they might be by social researchers are the *British Humanities Index* and the *Public Affairs Information Service Bulletin*. The former is published quarterly in the United Kingdom by the Library Association and its coverage includes not only most of the main social science journals but also serious weekly magazines, such as *The Economist* and *New Society*, and also *The Times*, the *Guardian* and other such popular publications; the latter is an American publication covering everything from books to articles and reports on all sorts of economic and social affairs published worldwide in the English language.

Newspapers are valuable sources of information, as has been noted, and it is a pity that *The Times* is the only British newspaper to have an index. This goes back to 1906, though indexes of different kinds are available back to 1790. A further source of information on current events is *Keesing's Contemporary Archives*, which is a weekly record of world events published in a loose-leaf format and available in most libraries. It is also well indexed on a weekly basis.

A very special index, for which some practice is needed

before it works properly, is the *Social Sciences Citation Index*. This American computer-produced service works from the principle that people with similar research interests who write articles cite the research of other people in their references. The *SSCI* is in three parts. The *Citation Index* looks at current publications to see what previously published articles are being cited by the present authors. This is organized alphabetically by authors being cited. Thus, if we know of an author who wrote a very good book or article a few years ago on our chosen topic we can look up his name to see if anyone has been citing that article recently. If someone has, then they must also have some interest in our interest. The *Source Interest* gives full details of the articles written by the people who have cited the people in the *Citation Index*. This information includes full author, title, journal, date, etc., as well as the place of work of the citing author. The third section of the *SSCI* is the *Permuterm Subject Index* in which keywords taken from journal article titles are paired and listed alphabetically. Thus, an article on working mothers and their relations with their daughters would appear under the heading of 'mothers' and be paired with 'working', 'relations' and 'daughters', and these words would appear again as starter keywords. The *Permuterm Index* can be very useful in locating work on topics for research, though many references one finds are not necessarily relevant.

Social researchers need also to be aware of the valuable information available from less formal published sources and here the *British Reports, Translations and Theses* is a self-explanatory title. Also, the British Library's *Index of Conference Proceedings Received*, which uses keywords for its indexing, can be invaluable. The Aslib *Index to British University Theses*, begun in 1950, includes all higher degrees in universities, polytechnics and with the CNAA, whilst *Dissertation Abstracts International* covers North American and some European theses.

The world of parliamentary publications in Britain is a

daunting one for the beginning researcher, but the range of information available from governmental and quasi-governmental sources is so vast that no researcher dare ignore it. The annual catalogue of Her Majesty's Stationery Office covers both parliamentary and non-parliamentary publications and there are also monthly and even daily lists to keep the information fresh, as well as sectional lists on particular governmental areas. Governmental statistics should be basic data for much social research and it is forunate that the Governmental Statistical Service publishes a free annual booklet called 'Government Statistics: a Brief Guide to Sources', which is available from the Central Statistical Office, Great George Street, London SW1P 3AQ. The major source, however, is the *Guide to Official Statistics*, begun in 1976, which has a very detailed index. All social researchers will benefit also from using *Social Trends*, which is published annually and is an excellent source book, interestingly produced, for a wide range of social topics.

From this brief résumé of the sources available to social researchers it should now be very clear that a vague wander through the bookshelves of the library is inefficient and time-wasting. Librarians have produced some magnificent bibliographical tools for the use of social researchers; they should be used more.[24]

CONCLUSIONS

Looking back over this chapter I am struck by the dreadful pitfalls which seem to beset every step which the sociologist might contemplate taking in documentary research. Against the naive assumption that if it says so in the book (or the paper, or the report) it must be true, we appear to have cast doubt on every type of written document ever produced. Documents are our (and other people's) history. They record events past, and the present stands in a causal relationship to the past. To ignore documents is to cut off sociology from the whole process of social change, which is one of the fundamental concepts of the discipline itself.

But documents can be dangerous things if used without care and if, as sometimes happens, they are used for partial and selective purposes. Every document has its contribution to make to research, but there may be other documents not used which could make their contribution too. The better researchers are acquainted with the bibliographical tools which can widen their perspectives, the better researchers they are likely to become.

5

People as Sources of Data

INTRODUCTION

A great deal of very useful research can be carried out wholly from documentary sources of one kind or another, but often social researchers find themselves in a position where they want to investigate social behaviour on which there is very little published research or perhaps what research has been published is not relevant enough to their own particular areas of interest. In my own studies of theatre audiences and of book reading habits in the United Kingdom I found, when I began, that there was very little published at all on who goes to the theatre[1] and, while there was more information available on adult reading habits, much of it had its source in America and much of what was available in Britain referred to borrowing from libraries but excluded book buying.

For many reasons, then, the social investigator may have to carry out his own observations to collect new data for his researches. Since Alexander Pope declared that 'the proper study of mankind is man' it would seem reasonable for social scientists to observe the behaviour of their fellow men and women. Much social behaviour can be observed without too much difficulty and people quite often enjoy talking and telling other people about their interests, so the researcher can often interview people too. To watch and to listen are two important activities for the social investigator studying social behaviour as it really happens.

But the social researcher is watching and listening (let us call them together observing) for a purpose, and that purpose is one of scientific enquiry. It is therefore necessary to use some sort of classification to sort out the various ways in which we might approach the problems of observation. One way is to use two factors, rather in the way that we did for documents, and these two factors will be called 'participation' and 'control'. Both of them can be thought of as being exercised in varying degrees, so that observation of people can be carried out with varying degrees of participation and varying degrees of control. Table 2 gives a general idea of the application of these two factors, and for illustrative convenience a two-by-two box has been constructed with four illustrative forms of observation in the boxes.

Table 2

Minimum	Participation		Maximum

Control	'Bird-watching'	Participant observation
	Laboratory observation	The interview

Maximum

By the term 'participation' is meant the degree of actual involvement of the observer in the situation under observation. Thus, when minimal participation takes place the observer keeps out of the group being studied as much as possible. In the ideal situation he is hidden completely from the observed, who are not aware of the researcher's presence at all. By contrast, when maximum participation is used, the observer is with and among the subjects of observation, as in the case of the interview situation where questions are asked and answers given.

By the term 'control' is meant the degree to which the observation is standardized in the interest of scientific accuracy. Thus, an observation would be relatively uncontrolled if the observer had no way of manipulating a social situation for the purposes of the enquiry. In the minimal situation of control, therefore, the observer would simply have to take things as they came. He would not be able to manipulate the situation at all. If observation is broken down into seeing and hearing this would mean that the observer watched or listened to (or both, of course) a social scene which was completely natural and unaffected by his presence. When degrees of control are introduced then the situation does become manipulated by the observer. The laboratory experiment is an obvious case of control, since a complete situation is created by and for the observer. In the situation of verbal interaction the observer intrudes control by means of standardized questions, perhaps standardized pre-set responses and pre-arranged classification for noting answers on a recording schedule.

Taking the two dimensions together and applying them, as above, in a four-fold scheme, produces what I have called the 'bird-watcher' method, the laboratory observation, participant observation and the standardized interview. These are merely convenient labels to attach to forms of observing people which in the actual live situation are unlikely to be found in a 'pure' form. Nevertheless, they are useful enough here to employ as starting points for an examination of ways in which real people can be studied by the social investigator.

'BIRD-WATCHING': UNCONTROLLED NON-PARTICIPANT

This could be described as 'pure' observation in that the observer does not participate in any way in the social interaction under observation and also does absolutely nothing to control the setting or the behaviour of the people observed. It is sometimes referred to as 'non-interventionist' observation, though I find that a rather jargonish term and I think bird-watching is a good simple way of referring to observation which is very similar to that of the ornithologist who constructs a 'hide' so as to be able to observe birds in their natural habitat without disturbing them in any way.

In social bird-watching it is very important that the people studied are not aware that they are being studied or that anyone is setting up a particular environment for them to behave in. Bird-watching has been used by many researchers to study children's behaviour. It can also be used to study people in their public leisure activities such as at football matches or in public houses. I have myself used this technique in the preparatory stages of researches in theatres, bookshops and libraries. The great advantage is that no external stimuli are applied to the subjects of the observation – all their actions and the situations they are in are absolutely normal. The disadvantages are the limitations that are placed on the observer who can only gain a limited amount of information without intruding and thus altering the spontaneity of the behaviour. For example, in one bookshop, just before Christmas, I saw two women examining books on football suitable for young people. Both spoke to each other in whispers. They clearly needed some help in deciding what book to buy, but they did not ask an assistant and eventually went out without purchasing. There were several questions I would have liked to have put to them, but had I done so I would have altered the environment for them and made them hyper-conscious of their limitations.

While bird-watching is often used at an early stage in research to try to develop hypotheses and to make sure one does have some idea of how people behave before going any further, there is no reason why one should not develop more systematic recording schedules to standardize the observations and to develop more of a survey approach. The observation schedule shown on pages 100 to 101 was used by students

Bookshop Schedule
Time observation began . . . . ended . . . . . .

Personal Details
Male □   Female □
Married □   Single □   Don't know □

Age estimate
Under 11 □
At school □
Student □
Under-20 worker □

20s □
30s □
40s □
50s □
60s+ □

Age guess

| 10 | 20 | 30 | 40 | 50 | 60 | 70 | 80 |

Occupation/Status . . . . Don't know □
Person alone □   with . . . . others
With whom? . . . .
Books bought . . . None □   Don't know □

Initial behaviour on entering shop . . . .
. . . .

Contact with assistants   None □
. . . .

Conversation with any other customers   None □
. . . .

Actual reading of books   None □   Time . . . . . .   Any details
. . . .

Detailed description of person (to amplify status) . . . .
. . . .

Place on continuum:

Purposive |————————————————| Browser

Sections visited	Time spent at each section	Observation of behaviour (e.g. reading, blurbs, last page, flicking through, possible attraction of author, subject, jacket)	Estimated no. of books looked at	Estimated no. of books chosen

during a day's observation of people in a bookshop and helped us to realize that the women shoppers were often much more purposive than the men in their bookshop behaviour. Clearly, though, the use of observation schedules is putting more control on the behaviour of the observer, so we may now turn to a consideration of what happens when we go further along that axis.

LABORATORY OBSERVATION: CONTROLLED NON-PARTICIPANT

In its ideal form this is observation carried out in an environment which may or may not be a natural one, but even if it is natural a situation has been deliberately created and is observed unbeknownst to the actors. One might say that the 'candid camera' technique used for some television programmes, where people have tricks played on them for the benefit of the viewers, is rather in this mode of observation, though it is to be hoped that social researchers would not encourage people to make fools of themselves in the way television producers do.

One technique which certainly creates a controlled environment is where laboratory or quasi-laboratory conditions are set up. In some cases people are invited into a laboratory and may be given tasks to carry out which may or may not be quite what they seem to be. There are numerous instances of volunteers being asked to do things (such as administering electric shocks to other people) which are really social situations deliberately created to test people's reactions to authority. Youth clubs may be organized on authoritarian or democratic lines to see how the members enjoy different forms of leadership. In simpler ways, libraries may deliberately remove certain reference works from their regular places on the shelves and then monitor reader reactions. (Sadly, readers often seem not to notice at all.) But any change in an organization or in a social setting can be used for controlled non-participant observation. The observer will need to be there observing, but possibly behind a hidden camera or watching through a one-way vision screen — he or she need not be in among the action. In market research what are called focus groups are sometimes used for initial exploratory discussions on new brands or new packaging under quasi-laboratory conditions. Perhaps eight people of various ages will be invited to an agency and will sit around in a comfortable room simply responding to very informal promptings from the discussion leader. But also there may be agency clients watching the participants from another room through a one-way screen to see and hear what the people do. In these circumstances it is more ethical to tell the participants about the screen. Hidden watchers and secret cameras do seem rather like the trappings of a police state and social researchers should not feel that they have a right to manipulate people.

PARTICIPANT OBSERVATION: NON-CONTROLLED PARTICIPANT

The term 'participant observation' is commonly used to describe rather different sorts of research methods, and in the very diffuseness of methods used under this umbrella term there lies a danger. Participant observation usually refers to a situation where the observer becomes as near as may be a member of the group being studied and participates in their normal activities. The term was originally used by Hader and Lindeman to refer to work done in industrial consultation committees where some members of the committee were trained to observe in detail what happened at meetings and were then questioned afterwards by research workers — rather like an intelligence officer might question the crew of an aircraft after a raid.[2] But the term has also been used to refer to the work done by anthropologists who have lived with tribes they have studied.

Writing on this method of enquiry, John Madge said that

'when the heart of the observer is made to beat as the heart of any other member of the group under observation, rather than as that of a detached emissary from some distant laboratory, then he has earned the title of participant observer.'[3] Madge's argument for the use of participant observation was that the ordinary interview situation is such a highly artificial social situation that both questioner and informant are in false positions. The interviewer is trying to be objective and scientific, yet has to establish and maintain 'rapport' if he is to get a good interview. The informant is trying to co-operate in this artificial situation, yet is being told to act and talk 'naturally'. If informant and observer lack a common purpose, the inferences made by the interviewer could be quite wrong. Far better to make sure that the inferences are correct, and this can be done by ensuring that the observer and the observed are thinking together, not in opposition.

Participant observation, then, is an attempt to put both observer and observed on the same side by making the former a member of the group so that he can experience what they experience and work within their frame of reference. Ideally, the participant observer is virtually a spy, since to be accepted completely in a particular capacity within a group the observer should be thought of as actually being in nothing but that capacity. It is on this point that participant observation in practice very often does not match up to the ideal form and some consideration should be given to the situation arising.

Perhaps the easiest way to consider the range of behaviour under the umbrella term 'participant observation' is to separate the words 'observer' and 'participant' and think of four possibilities – a complete observer, an observer as participant, a participant as an observer and a complete participant. The 'complete observer' is really a bird-watcher by another name and as such has already been dealt with. The 'observer as participant' is known by the group under study to be an observer but has been accepted, temporarily, by the group and allowed temporary membership to enable him to carry out the research. Perhaps the classic case of this sort was William Foot Whyte's study *Street Corner Society* where he became a quasi-gang member but never lost his status of researcher.[4] Very often social anthropologists who study primitive tribes 'live' with them for a period of time using this role. The people of the tribe or village agree to them participating in their lives to some extent but there is no pretence that the lady from America has actually become a Polynesian native. In the famous Middletown studies made by Robert and Helen Lynd the Lynds lived for a time in Muncie, Indiana, but were always known to be researchers.[5] Clearly, a great advantage of this particular type of participant observation is that the researchers are in the group or community and can quite openly ask as many questions as they feel necessary. The limitation is that the people under observation may well feel rather acutely that they are being observed and may react against the observers, act unnaturally and perhaps even lie.

The next step, that of being 'participant as an observer', requires observers to adopt roles which enable them to become a member of a group and yet to be able to ask questions without fully disclosing their roles as researchers. This is a position which requires the researcher to adopt a false role, for example, pretending to be an author looking for atmosphere for a book or pretending to be a management trainee with a firm. Both these roles would allow the researcher to seem inquisitive and to ask questions without the members of the group knowing the true nature of the work the researcher was doing. A young research social scientist could well go into a factory and tell the people she worked with that she was a student on a placement for, say, three months, learning about the realities of factory work, when in fact she was a graduate research worker carrying out a carefully planned study of labour–management relationships. The role enables the researcher to gain the confidence of the group that accepts her in her false role.

The extreme form of participant observation — what I have called the 'complete participant' — is, in fact, typified by the spy, who is believed by members of the group to be a genuine member of that group and is not known to be an observer at all. This extreme role can be used to try to understand extreme situations. John Howard Griffin made himself up to look like a negro and passed himself off as one in the southern USA for his book *Black Like Me.*[6] Tony Wilkinson dressed up as a down-and-out in London and lived like a tramp for several weeks as part of a television enquiry into London's dossers, published in book form as *Down and Out.*[7] Both men took grave risks in the roles they adopted and could well have been attacked had their disguises been broken by the people they lived with. Interestingly, neither of these two people were sociologists, though sociologists have carried out participant studies amongst homosexuals and criminal gangs. The technique, however, is not new and Keating's *Into Unknown England, 1866–1913* contains several fascinating accounts of similar participant studies by social observers of the nineteenth century in workhouses and cheap lodging houses.[8] The most serious problem about complete participation is a moral one rather than a practical one. Whatever one may argue for the value of research findings which ensue from this technique (and certainly the publication of *Down and Out* must have come as a revelation to many people in present-day Britain) the question must be squarely faced as to whether the social researcher has a right to deceive and manipulate people for research purposes. Tramps and dossers are not likely to organize a powerful protest lobby to Parliament to complain about intrusion into their private lives and criminals are even less likely to take legal action (though they will consider illegal retaliation). This extreme role really depends upon the social researcher deciding whether the means are justified by the ends. Personally, I did once use such a role, while an undergraduate, working in a factory on a vacation research project. At the time I had few qualms and found the role-playing exciting;

today I feel I was condescending to the people I deceived and I would not do it again.

THE INTERVIEW:
CONTROLLED PARTICIPATION

In social research the term 'interview' is used to describe a wide range of differing things and it is best to begin with a simple definition which focuses on the essential meaning of the word. The *Shorter Oxford Dictionary* defines 'interview' as 'a meeting of persons face to face, especially for the purpose of formal conference on some point'. The interview is basically a form of human interaction and may range from the most informal chat to the most carefully pre-coded and carefully systematized set of questions and answers laid out on an interview schedule.

All sociologists whose work takes them out of the library and brings them into contact with living beings are certain to use the interview in their work. John Madge made a useful distinction between various sorts of people who may be the subject for the sociologist's interview. The 'potentate' may have to be interviewed to obtain permission and goodwill to carry out a study in the institution he controls, such as a factory, office, school or youth club. The 'expert' may have to be interviewed because she has special knowledge of a situation which it is vital for the researcher to have guidance on. In these interview situations, as Madge carefully pointed out, there are special circumstances operating and special precautions to be taken by the interviewer.

It is not uncommon for potentates to be experts as well and, in my experience, it is very important for a researcher to establish goodwill with people who will he helping in a research project. For example, when I began researching into social aspects of book reading I knew very little at all about publishing or bookselling and my experience of libraries was mainly limited to being a user of them. It was important to learn about, for example, bookselling from experienced booksellers who then, accepting the genuineness of my interest and the possible value of my research, were generous in helping me with it and allowing me to carry out surveys in bookshops. In a research project I carried out into academic publishing a great deal of the work required me to interview very experienced and knowledgeable publishers and to ask questions which, inevitably, touched on financial matters. In practically every case the publishers were prepared to supply me with information which was not generally made public. In some cases I had to accept that information given to me to help me understand problems of academic publishing was to remain confidential, but once credibility had been established the publishers were very helpful.

It is sometimes difficult for research workers from an academic background to convince businessmen and other such people of the value of their research. To a publisher or bookseller working hard to make a living in a very chancy occupation time spent answering questions from a researcher who has never himelf worked in a commercial business may seem to be time wasted. It is incumbent upon the researcher to explain clearly at the very onset why the research is being done, what sort of results are hoped for and what feedback there is likely to be which may help the potentate and/or expert who has helped with the project. Research studies which may seem quite practical to university people may seem very far removed from reality to practitioners, and research workers who are prepared to learn from the practitioners can often modify their research plans and greatly improve them. This is not to say that the researcher simply becomes the handmaid of the practitioner; it is merely that the researcher who is not prepared to learn from the practitioner is arrogant and lacking in insight.

Of course, experts do tend to have their personal biases and the researchers must be cautious about what they accept as information from the people they interview. If everyone in, say, librarianship, was agreed on the best way to organize library services there would be little need for research, for conferences or for journals and books on librarianship. Experts can be fallible and usually the best practitioners are the people who, with experience, come to appreciate how little they know. They are the ones who are usually prepared to co-operate with, and to help, research workers: people who are so expert that they know all the answers have no perception of the value of research. The interview, then, is a most valuable tool for the researcher worker and to be able to deal competently with potentates and experts is of the greatest importance.

But many interviews carried out in social research are of samples of what we might call 'ordinary' people – people who have characteristics, opinions and knowledge of a much more general nature. Here one could instance people who go to the theatre as opposed to theatre administrators, people who read books rather than people in publishing, selling or lending. We can obtain information from people such as these by asking questions. This can be done by asking them to complete questionnaries for us or talk to us. At this stage we are concerned with the personal touch; self-completed questionnaires will be dealt with later. By interviewing people we can obviously obtain a great deal of information in a relatively short time. What is the main point of the interview?

Perhaps the best way to approach the interview is to consider first what stage the research has reached. If we are at an early stage of the work, still looking around for ideas and still perhaps 'hypothesis-seeking', it is likely that we shall want to talk to people to try to get help, stimulation, new viewpoints, and so on. It seems rather grandiose to label a talk with a colleague in the same office or department as an 'interview', but in some ways it could be considered to be one, especially if our colleague is an expert in the field in which we ourselves have become interested. But usually we think of the early idea-seeking interview as being with a non-expert, an 'ordinary' person who does not have any particular consultant status. The position can be illustrated simply by thinking of a study that is to take place of the social workings of a youth club to test out some hypothesis about the manifest and latent functions of this association. Obviously we would have to be prepared to see the potentates who control the club to obtain permission to work in it. We would almost certainly have talks with the club leader, the expert, for his knowledge and views. But the 'ordinary' people in this case would be the members of the club itself, and we would probably be thinking of testing our hypotheses by interviewing a sample of the club members.

The main point here, then, is that the expert is interviewed as an individual with special knowledge. The ordinary people are interviewed because they are representatives of the group which we are studying, and as such their characteristics, opinions, and so on are only of interest because they can be added together to present the general picture of the group itself. To interview only one club member and then say that he could be taken as representative of the whole club membership — perhaps several hundred in number — could not be substantiated. But on the other side, it is not necessary to interview everyone in the club if the proper statistical sampling rules are obeyed and if proper tests of significance are applied to results obtained. The sample survey is a fully recognized method of enquiry in common everyday use by sociologists, economists, psychologists, public opinion pollsters, market researchers and many other bodies. The sort of interviews to be used will depend largely on the theoretical orientation of the survey being made. The market research survey to find out what brand of toothpaste housewives prefer is not likely to be based on very much sociological theory. A survey of the mental image of the sausage among housewives (this example is not made up) may use psychological *techniques* but is unlikely to be tied up with much basic psychological theory. Consumer surveys rarely go beyond the practical aims of the people who commission (and pay for) them. However, many market research studies are carried out on large samples which would be beyond the reach of academic researchers and it is not unusual to find commercial surveys which contain quite valuable social information. The government itself, of course, through its own various research organizations, and especially in Britain the Office of Population Censuses and Surveys, carries out a great deal of valuable social research based on interviewing.

In our consideration of the interview for scientific enquiry we must always remind ourselves that the survey is merely a particular tool for collecting information which is deemed relevant for the testing of a hypothesis which stems from theory. The sociologically based interview has thus rather more to it than merely being a test of the reaction to Brand X. Here a difficulty does arise though, and it is best to face up to it right away. Many people carry out interviews and write them up from a social point of view. Newspaper reporters do this all the time and what is often these days called 'investigative journalism' may use teams of interviewers who together write up full-page reports on chosen topics. Books, too, use the results of interviews to give 'human interest'. Often the interviews are very readable material indeed. But they are not sociology. The newspaper reporters, the commercial writers and the popularizers may have great social insight and great interviewing skills, but their work is very likely to be strongly value-laden and biased and they are not working for the development of sociological theory. With this in mind one can see, then, that for the purposes of *sociological* enquiry the form of the interview must always be ultimately referable to its value in the advancement of sociological theory.

It is not necessary always to think of the interview as only of the highly standardized sample type. It may well be that a particular piece of research needs to focus on selected people for information, and the information gained from them will be fitted together into a coherent and consistent pattern with virtually no percentages and significance tests at all. This sort of interviewing could well be characteristic of a community survey where the researcher went from person to person linking up kinship networks, occupational groups, recreational groups, religious bodies, and so on. The people interviewed would not be experts, but would simply be key participants with useful knowledge, whose interviews would yield far more useful information than a random survey of the community. In particular, if a historical perspective enters into the survey it may well be quite invaluable to interview old people for their memories of the community as it was so many years ago. In recent years the development of oral history has resulted in many interviews with older people being tape-recorded for the development of sound archives. One example of this work is the taped interviews carried out for the Imperial War Museum in London of the remaining survivors of the 1914-18 war. Local historians and rural sociologists too are making greater use of this oral approach.

If what has just been said gives an impression that interviews can be almost infinite in their variety, perhaps this is not a bad thing. Certainly, the standardized interview as used in a carefully conducted sample survey is important, but there are many other instances outside the sample survey in which the interview is an important research tool.

So let us consider what might be called the continuum of control in the interview situation; the one end of the continuum where there is the minimal amount of control can be called the situation of the 'informal interview' and the other end, where there is maximum control, may be called the 'formal interview'. This way of describing interviews can be used to consider what the control is exercised over, and where the types of interviews can most usefully be employed.

INFORMAL INTERVIEWS

The most informal interview will be one where the interviewer, having once started the interview off on the theme in which he is interested, allows the informant to dictate the subsequent situation. The interviewer is likely to start with some ideas to stimulate the informant to talk but beyond this he or she simply listens. Since an interview is essentially a stimulus-response situation this means that there is very little standardization of either the stimuli or the recording of the responses. For instance, if the interviewer is carrying out an interview with an old inhabitant of a village to try to find out what the community life was like 50 years ago he will probably have a set of categories for enquiry. Work, leisure, social stratification, social control, patterns of family life, the Church, and so on will be likely headings used to stimulate the respondent to talk about the past. Obviously these categories could be introduced very simply into the interview and the informant would just relate the memories which came back to him or her. A technique such as this was used by Blythe in his well-known village study of *Akenfield*.[9] The problem of how to record all the informant said would be best dealt with by means of a tape recorder so that the complete verbatim record could be kept and referred to when needed later. Otherwise, if the interviewer does not have shorthand, some form of selective recording (probably using a great deal of individual abbreviations) is needed. I have myself used this technique on a number of occasions in both urban and book research. One set of interviews, with the literary editors of national newspapers, was carried out using half a dozen 'topic headings' simply to ensure that at each interview I covered the ground I had decided beforehand was important for my purpose. In the interviews themselves the topics sometimes came up in different sequences according to the way that the particular interview developed. This did not matter, since it was the topics that counted, not the order of them or the way they were introduced. I did not use a tape recorder for these interviews, though one might have been helpful in some ways, though perhaps inhibiting to my informants in other ways. I had blank sections under my topic headings on paper in which I wrote very brief notes at the time and these were expanded more fully immediately after the interviews while my memory was still fresh. It must be admitted, though, that this very informal technique does require quite a lot of work to be done both before and especially after the interview and the researcher is always in danger of forgetting to put a point forward or not being able to understand his or her own notes afterwards.

Given these 'administrative' problems of the informal interview, what advantages and disadvantages does it have? One obvious advantage is that, as a social situation, the informal interview is very natural; the conversation flows much more like two people with a common interest having a talk together. There is not the amount of direct questioning that could give an interview the air of a lawyer/witness relationship. Informants have a great deal more liberty to range as they wish and to develop their ideas, and this 'freedom to roam' can be extremely useful in getting to the bottom of complex social situations and events. Rather than just giving a 'yes' or 'no' to a carefully put question from the interviewer the informant can control much more the direction of the discussion and can therefore decide what is or is not relevant to a particular situation. This enables the interviewer to burrow much further into the complexities of some situations and may well introduce him to relevant factors which had not been thought of before at all. When these new factors are brought out by the informant the interviewer can then follow them up in more detail by a simple prompt, such as 'Tell me more about what happened when the old vicar died and this new man came who fell out with the schoolmaster.' Given such prompts, some informants may then go on for hours with their recollections and reminiscences.

At its most extreme limits of informality the interview could be carried out with the interviewer taking no notes or tape recording at all. In this form the interview would be as near as possible to a personal discussion between two people with a common interest. It is sometimes suggested that the absence of note-taking can be a help to the informant, in that it frees him from the inhibiting effects of a recorder and a notebook. But, on the other hand, the informant who sees the interviewer making no record of what is said is just as likely to wonder why notes are *not* being taken. If what he has to say is worth hearing, why isn't the interviewer recording what he says? There is no evidence that research is at all hampered by note-taking, and many interviews of a very personal kind are carried out using tape recorders or notebooks.

Undoubtedly, then, the informal interview can produce fascinating results, and the interviewer can gain real depth of insight into what may be very complex social situations. The disadvantages, however, stem from the limitations of this form of interview as a scientific tool. In the informal interview it is apparent that a great deal depends on the skill of the interviewer, and perhaps two interviewers might get different responses from the same person in interviews purporting to cover the same topics. People can relatively easily be stimulated to talk about things in a particular way. For example, if a person is being asked about her educational background one interviewer could encourage her to talk about the criticisms she could offer of it, while another interviewer could concentrate on the benefits she received from it. On matters where there are social inhibitions about declaring one's most personal views or experiences, such as in sexual matters, family relationships, social class, religion and perhaps politics, it is obvious that informal interviewing could result in very selective discussions taking place from which the researcher would simply produce the sort of information which suited his own bias. It would not be difficult to conduct an informal interview with almost anyone, asking them for criticisms of the national health service, the police or the railways, all three of which confer great benefit on the population, for which they do not always receive much credit.

The informal interview, then, is open to question in a number of ways. If others came along and interviewed the same people on the same topics, would they get the same responses? Has the interviewer used the framework of informality to 'load' the interviews in a particular way? How can we be sure that the topics were put to a number of people in the same way; that is, were they all responding to the same stimuli? How much of what the informants said was discarded by the interviewer because he did not find it useful — and by what criteria did he decide what was useful and what was not? One particularly searching way of appraising informal interviews is to ask ourselves how much we accept what the interviewer tells us simply because it fits in with our own preconceptions or biases. If we find that, on the basis of informal interview, the writer is telling us that all working-class men love their employers dearly, or that working-class girls at grammar schools have no divided loyalties, do we accept these claims or dismiss them? The problem is obviously one of deciding how to appraise the evidence presented to us, and the difficulty of the informal interview is that it is so hard to appraise. In many cases we are virtually being asked to accept the evidence because the writer is putting it to us in a very skilful, persuasive way. But the good research worker is not wooed by skilled writing, by particular ideologies or by any other obvious bias, no matter how tempting they may be. Good social researchers are sceptical (in a healthy way) and take nothing on trust. They must be convinced by the evidence.

How, then, can the informal interview be used in sociology in an acceptable way? Two particular functions seem to suit the informal interview. First, it is an invaluable *exploratory* technique. In the early stages of an enquiry sociologists need to find out as much as possible about the situation or group which they intend to study. If they formulate detailed hypotheses and produce elaborate questionnaires or interview schedules without first carrying out informal interviews they may well go off in a completely fruitless direction and have only themselves to blame when they end up with several hundred completed forms, none of which have asked the right questions about the right key factors. Researchers are usually outsiders to the situations they study. Straight observation, participant observation and informal interviews can all help them to gain a better insight into the chosen field of enquiry. To neglect these techniques is to neglect the possibilities of a deeper, truer understanding of a situation. To rush in and quantify a situation which one does not understand is wasteful of the time of both researchers and informants. The informal interview cannot generally be used to *test* hypotheses very accurately, but it can be used most fruitfully to clarify them and to elaborate them.

The second role of the informal interview can be in an enquiry where the researcher is engaged in exploratory work, often of an academic type. Here one is dealing with social situations which are relatively unexplored and where sample surveys may be quite inappropriate. One piece of research which I contemplated some years ago, but did not actually carry out, was a comparison between people who do go to the theatre and those who do not. Sample surveys had shown that most people who go to the theatre tend to be middle-class and well-educated, but since so few people altogether actually go to the serious theatre there must be many middle-class, well-educated people who are not theatre-goers. How, then, do the two sorts of people differ from each other? Do they have different sorts of values and ideas? Do they have different social and cultural interests in other areas of life? The list of possible differences is quite fascinating. One *could* put all these postulated differences down on paper and, taking samples of the two groups, go off and interview them with all sorts of yes/no questions. But this, I suggest, would be crude and unfruitful. Had I gone on with this research at the depth which I had in view I would undoubtedly have used a far more informal interview and, having chosen possible points of difference, I would have introduced these in the interviews and let the informants develop the themes themselves. Undoubtedly, some of my own ideas would have been useless and other ideas would have suggested themselves during the interviews. To convince the reader of my findings in any subsequent report on the study I would have had to show that the points made by my informants did produce a coherent and logical pattern. This is not an easy concept to put over, but the analogy of the case presented in the criminal court may be used to illustrate it. The jurymen are asked to hear the evidence and on the basis of the evidence to decide whether or not they think the prosecution have proved, beyond reasonable doubt, that Mr X was drunk in charge, or whatever the crime may be. In the case of the evidence produced by informal interviews we, the readers, are rather in the position of hearing a case put by only one counsel and not the other. The researcher who 'attacks' a social situation would be the prosecution, the researcher who 'defends' would obviously be the defence counsel. We, as jurymen, must listen to one set of evidence only and be prepared to do our own mental cross-examination. Like all analogies, this one can mislead as well as help, but if we do feel that a reasonable case is being presented to us, and that the internal evidence of the research fits together coherently and comes to a result which is 'beyond reasonable doubt' then we may be prepared to accept this piece of research, based though it is on informal interviews.

But two other things can happen. We may find that the writer was completely biased in his views and that he falsified his evidence, in which case he is a perjurer and we should hold him in contempt. Second, we may find that other research refutes the findings of the first study. In this case we must reconstitute ourselves into a court of appeal and go through all the evidence afresh.

The problems of the informal interview, then, are considerable, and they may make us feel that the formal type of interview is much less beset with difficulties and open to the criticism of lack of scientific method. To see whether this is really so we will, in the next chapter, consider the problems which arise in the use of the formal interview.

6

The Sample Survey with Formal Interviews

INTRODUCTION

The term 'formal interview' is used here to designate a type of interview in which there is an appreciable amount of control exercised over both the presentation of the questions (stimuli) and the recording of the answers (responses). In this method of interviewing it is likely that the hypotheses will have been clarified so that specific questions are ready for testing, and an interview schedule is to be used so that the stimulus-response situation of the interview can be standardized for a number of interviewers. The answers received will be analysed in tabular form for statistical presentation and so categories of response must be considered at a relatively early stage. In all, the questions will be governed much more by problems of standardization and quantification.

In doing this it is likely that much of the richness of the uncontrolled interview will be lost, but the aims of the formal interview are not richness, rather they are uniformity of question from a team of fieldworkers, and rapid quantification of answers for analysis and testing. The two types of interview are by no means in opposition; they are different tools for different tasks. The human element which is so much a part of the informal approach must be standardized if a team is to operate as a unit. The individual interview situations will cease to be case studies and will become units of a sample.

It should be noted before going any further that for a sample survey to be of any value at all the sampling procedure must be open to scrutiny and stand up to criticism. We shall, therefore, now briefly consider some of the basic issues involved in sampling for social surveys before considering the interview schedules used in them.

SAMPLING

If we want to collect information about some aspect or aspects of a large group (whether the group is made up of people or things) the obvious approach would appear to be a survey of all of them. But in many real-life situations it is not possible to collect information about every case — or the whole 'population', as we call it. For example, a manufacturer of upholstery fabric may want to know how well his cloth wears, so he gives a certain piece of the cloth a standardized 'rubbing' test to see how many rubs it can stand before wearing through. If the manfacturer did this test on every yard of cloth he made he would be left with only worn-out cloth for sale. A wholesale buyer of women's underwear for a large store could not hope to inspect every single item she intends buying; what she usually does is to inspect a sample of goods and to base her decision on this. Conversely, the stallholder in the fruit and vegetable market who puts all his best tomatoes at the front of the pile and then fills the customer's bag with soft squelchy ones from the back is deliberately showing the purchaser a false sample. Practially every day in one way or another we carry out some form of sampling for ourselves in our ordinary daily round.

We may find ourselves disagreeing with other people on the basis of sampling; one man may claim that a shirt he bought from a well-known manufacturer wore out in no time at all, whereas his friend says he always buys this make because they wear so well. Probably the first person got an unfortunate sample. We may generalize from very limited samples: for example we may say, echoing the words of Michael Flanders' and Donald Swann's lovely song of patriotic prejudice that the Irishman 'sleeps in his boots and lies in his teeth', that the Welshman is 'dishonest, little and dark — more like monkey than man' or that the Scotsman is 'mean, bony, blotchy and covered with hair'. But such generalizations as these, while perhaps being applicable to a few individuals of each country, can reasonably be said to be prejudiced statements based on inadequate sampling.

Today, the importance of *good* sampling becomes more important as more and more surveys are carried out on sample bases. Sampling saves time, labour and, therefore, money and by reducing the numbers of cases involved it allows for a concentration of effort on high quality information about the smaller number of cases involved. But it must be recognized at the outset that as soon as sampling is carried out the statements made about the cases involved become *probability* statements. Sampling must mean abandoning certainty for probability, but this is not any great problem if sampling is correctly carried out, since the margins of probable error can be calculated in many instances.

AVOIDING BIAS BY RANDOM SAMPLING

Bias is a problem in all aspects of social research and no more important a case of bias problems can be found than in sampling. Most samples are based on the concept of 'random sampling', so it is important to understand what is meant by the word 'random'. Yule and Kendall say that 'the selection of an individual from a population is random when each member of the population has the same chance of being chosen.' This is a useful definition because it stresses the basic point of everyone (or everything) having the same chance. One can see from this that random sampling is not at all the same as what we might call 'personal choice'. If I were to ask a school-teacher to choose for me a sample which she considered to be a fair cross-section of her pupils so that I could interview them for a survey, there would almost certainly be a personal bias in the sample given to me. I might well never find out where it was, but it would certainly contain some pupils whom the teacher had chosen because she thought they were bright and co-operative and others would almost certainly have been excluded because of their uncooperativeness or lower intelligence. Selection of this sort raises all kinds of problems of the sample being consciously or unconsciously affected by the selector's personal biases.

A further problem of bias comes when the total group (or 'sample frame') from which the sample is taken is inadequate. A simple example may be used here. Suppose one wants to take a sample of full-time students of a university. Whatever actual technique we use for taking the sample the key thing is that everyone should be 'on the list' in the first place. If a faculty, or department, or a certain special group of students is missed out then the sample itself has not been drawn from the correct population. This could happen, for instance, if one were using faculty lists of students as the sample frame and there were certain students in special departments who were not in any faculty. Students away from the university, say on a sandwich course or having a year abroad, might or might not be included in lists one used.

Suppose, though, that we wanted a sample of a rather more difficult group. It is very difficult to sample young people in the general population, since there is no list of them anywhere. For adults over the age of 18 the electoral roll is the normal sample frame, but even this is far from perfect since it is compiled only once each year and many people fail to fill in the necessary forms while others may change address shortly after registering. For young people under 18 the problem is tremendous, since to compile a list of such people would require a complete canvas of an area simply asking at every house for details of the under-18s. In Schofield's pioneering study of the sexual behaviour of young people he was primarily interested in those between 15 and 19 years of age and he faced this very problem.[1] In one area he was fortunate enough to gain access to doctors' lists, which contain the names of most of the population since nearly everyone of every age is registered with a general practitioner. But this list was denied hin in other areas and he then used school lists, projecting forward for the people who had left school; but this had many errors and losses, with people moving home. In another area he did actually get a market research firm's fieldworkers to go round all the houses asking for young men and women in the age group, and while this appeared to give a reasonably accurate sample frame it was also very expensive. Market research companies will, of course, undertake to survey special groups of almost any kind, but the costs of finding, for example, people who have recently bought double-glazing or read romantic novels can be very high.

This point leads on to a further problem in sampling — which is non-response. Sampling from out-of-date lists results in large numbers of people who cannot be found. Questionnaires sent by post are not returned and interviews are refused. All these factors reduce the response rate, no matter how good the original sample may have been, so that what may have been a reasonable one-in-five sample to begin with ends up as nearer one-in-ten actually obtained, because of losses. Here the great problem is to try to decide if the non-respondents differ in any way from the respondents and of course in most cases they obviously do in not being interested in the subject of the survey itself.

In all these ways, then, sampling has its problems and bias must be guarded against at every step. Some ways of sampling will now be considered.

Steps in sampling

Let us begin by considering how we might obtain a random sample; that is, one in which each member of the population has the same chance of being chosen. Probably we have in our mind's eye something in the nature of a raffle as being a form of random sampling, and we are right in thinking of this as one method. The raffle or lottery is a form of random sample — in its simplest form the identical little numbered tickets are shaken up in a hat and drawn out one by one by someone with their eyes closed. In the case of the 'draw' for the Football Association Cup numbered balls are drawn from a bag and each number indicates a club. At a more sophisticated level the British premium bond machine ERNIE (electronic random number indicator equipment) is a raffle on a large scale. The ERNIE machine is a modern computerized form of sampling by 'random numbers' which has been used for many years in research. In the original method the total units were given numbers from 1 upwards and the sample taken by means of tables of random numbers which could be bought. For instance, suppose we want to take a random sample of ten students from a class of 50. We could, as in a lottery, put each name on a piece of card, all cards being identical, put them into a hat, shake well and take out ten cards. By using random numbers we could do the job almost the other way round, by using a list of numbers already randomized for us. This way we would give each student on our list a two-digit number, from 01 to 50, and then run through a page of random numbers, using them in two-digit sets, until we had got ten within the range of 01 to 50. In the table below we would, working downwards, get the numbers 29, 41, 23, 5, 27, 7, 25, 35, 3, and 8.

2952	9792	7979	7002	8126
4167	2762	7203	5911	6111
2370	6107	3563	5356	3170
0560	9025	6008	1089	1300

(The above twenty sets of four digits are taken from L. H. C. Tippett's *Random Sampling Numbers* which gives a further 10,380 sets.)

It can be seen that a long list of students (or any other units) could be used for a random sample by this means simply by numbering from beginning to end, and this could be done with an automatic increasing numbering stamp. The rule is simply that one uses as many digits as are in the final number (three digits if in hundreds, four if in thousands, and so on) and then uses the random numbers in appropriate sets. Since books of random numbers contain thousands of sets of figures and one can work up, down, or across, since all is random, there is no problem of running short of numbers.

It may seem that the above methods are too time-consuming when one could just as well take every *n*th name from the list for one's sample. In the case of the ten out of 50 students, why not just think of a number from one to ten and then take every tenth name from there on? This is what Moser calls 'quasi-random' sampling in that it is almost but not quite random.[2] The main reason why it is not completely random is that one cannot be sure in every list that the *n*th name does not have some significance. It could be, for instance, that every tenth house in a street coincides with a building plan which has larger houses at intervals and these are over-sampled. It might be that in a list of names every tenth name is the leader of a section of ten people; to sample by every tenth would then result in either a sample of nothing but leaders or a sample with no leaders at all. The point is that regular-interval sampling makes every case dependent upon the first choice and so each individual unit does not have the same chance of being sampled. It may also be noted that if this method is employed then the *first* number chosen should be by random means rather than just 'saying a number between 1 and 10' since it is well known that choices between these limits do not come out anything like randomly — the number 7 being particularly popular.

So far we have considered three ways of sampling directly from a given population, but it may be thought that this direct method has dangers attached. After all, if we want a representative sample of university students we may already know how they are distributed between departments or faculties and random methods, being based on chance, might now and then produce samples heavily biased towards one faculty. Our supposed sample of university students might, just by chance, turn out to be nearly all from the faculty of law, which may be only a very small faculty. To safeguard against this sort of distortion, yet without basically interfering with our random system, we can build in a sort of screening device which is called stratification.

Stratification

With many populations we are already aware that the units fall into sub-groups of which we would wish to take account in any sampling. For example, in our group of students we would almost certainly know what sex they were, and we may feel that our sample of 1 in 5 should reflect this fact. Put in the very simplest way then, suppose the group was 30 males and 20 females, our stratified sample would be 6 males and 4 females. We would take 6 men at random from the 30 men, and 4 women at random from the 20 women. Stratification safeguards the representativeness of the sample by ensuring that the known groups in the population are represented fairly in the sample. This is not a departure from random methods since these are used within the strata; it is simply a job done beforehand as a precaution against freak random results *if* the distribution of the special factors in the population is accurately known beforehand. It can be seen that comparisons between the sub-groups are made much easier if they have been sampled in this way; there is no problem of having to cope with a preponderance of one group and a dearth of another if stratification has taken place beforehand.

Multi-stage sampling

There is a further way of sampling, using a certain amount of ordering of the units before sampling takes place. Multi-stage sampling can be used when the population is made up of a number of sub-units. Perhaps a military rather than an educational example is the simplest to use here. One may think of an army brigade as being composed of battalions, battalions made up of companies and companies made up of platoons. If one wanted to take a sample of soldiers in a particular brigade simple random sampling could mean finding a large number of individual soldiers randomly across their various units. 'Multi-stage sampling helps to concentrate the work on a limited number of groups by sampling groups first before the individuals are reached.' Thus, one could take a random sample of the battalions first and then on through the companies and platoons until the actual individual soldiers were sampled only from a limited number of platoons instead of from the whole brigade. 'It is important to note that a presupposition of this sort of sampling is that each stage is composed of similar sub-units so that sampling at each stage will not result in unrepresentative samples.' This presupposes a homogeneity of units which cannot always be supported in fact, but the individual investigator must take decisions on this problem in each case as it arises.

Cluster sampling

A further way of reducing the spread of sampling is to use what is called cluster sampling, a device by which sub-units are grouped together and work concentrated on them. A simple example in the case of the university student population would be to take the faculties of the university (let us say there are then, just for example) and take a sample of two of them. These two faculties, randomly chosen, would then be used for the sample with perhaps all the students, or a high proportion of them, being the sample. One can see at once the problem here is whether the faculties of, say, medicine and engineering are a good cross-section of the university. For some purposes they might be, for others (particularly in their general lack of women students) they could be quite misleading. But cluster sampling does have value when distance may provide real obstacles to conducting enquiries. So a survey of an area such as a city might raise genuine problems of getting about to see people, and cluster sampling might sample a number of polling districts and concentrate the interviews in them to the complete exclusion of all the other polling districts. The great danger of cluster sampling is that one must be able to take the clusters together as a total unit if they are to be used for anything more than just cluster comparisons. It is very difficult at times to say whether the clusters do really add up to a representation of the whole. One can see that cluster sampling of a city's schools might result in a complete set of working-class schools with no middle-class ones at all; or even completely middle- with no working-class. If there *is* prior knowledge of such problems selection along stratification lines is probably preferable.

Quota sampling

This type of sampling has given rise to quite a lot of criticism when used for political poll surveys. As can be imagined, trying to obtain reasonable samples of the general population for relatively short interviews on such topics as voting behaviour or food preferences can result in a lot of interviewers having to call at a lot of houses over all towns and cities in the country. How much simpler to station an interviewer at a busy part of a town and have her interview people who are passing by. But obviously we know that interviewers simply given the task of producing say 20 interviews might choose only women of a fairly young age-group and we know this is not representative of the population. So we can actually lay down certain guidelines, rather like stratified samples, telling the interviewers that so many interviews should be with men and so many with women, so many in certain age-groups and perhaps so many in certain pre-determined socio-economic groups. Since the sex, age and social class distributions for the general population are known it is not difficult to parcel out the interviewers' tasks according to these criteria. So each interviewer goes out hunting for informants who fit into the right boxes — or quotas. These quota controls, as they are called, can be independent or interrelated. In the former case the interviewer may have to find 10 men and 10 women, and these 20 must be composed of 6 under 30, 7 between 30 and 55 and 7 over 55.

But sex and age controls do not operate *together* on any one interview. So long as the 20 completed interviews fit these two controls all is well. But if the controls are interrelated then the 20 cases will be divided into 10 men and 10 women and for each sex the age groups will be specified. In this way the interviewer knows she must include, say, three women over 55. If a further control, such as social class, is added then interrelated controls can make the specifications very limited — the interviewer having to find two women aged 30 to 55, of lower middle-class — towards the quota of 20. Obviously, independent controls make life easier for interviewers, and interrelated controls make for more definitely representative samples. Quota sampling has the attaction of being easier, quicker and cheaper than actual house-to-house calls but there are distinct limitations which reduce its value. One snag is that some statistical tests, especially calculations of sample error, cannot be made on quota sampling because they are not based on *random* sampling. Further problems are particularly human ones which result in interviewers 'bending' information so as to fill quotas. Interviewers cannot be sure of people's age or social class before an interview is begun and so one can see the temptation of putting a woman down as under 35 if that is just what you need at the end of a hard day when the woman turns out in fact to be 38. A further problem of the street quota system is that people on the busiest streets are not always a good sample of the general population. Bus drivers and conductors resting between journeys are an obvious target for quota samples and are commonly over-represented as an occupation in such samples.

Panels

Rather than having to go out to find people and ask them to be interviewed or to complete questionnaires, it may seem very attractive to have them safely on a panel where they can be used when needed. Where information, particularly of a detailed nature, is to be collected over a period of time the panel has clear attractions. Both market research and government survey units use consumer panels of housewives for budget enquiries, finding out what the housewife spends on what over a given period by means of a diary of spending. Usually panel members of this sort are paid a certain sum of money for their trouble, but not enough to affect their standard of living and relevant purchases. The panel system is also used by audience research for their reactions to radio and television programmes. People are recruited for listening and viewing panels in the various regions and are stratified according to certain known characteristics such as sex, age and social class. The panel members then receive regular questionnaires asking for their opinions of selected pro-grammes over the past week. These panels are likely to suffer from what has been called 'duty' listening or viewing in which a person feels he or she *ought* to, say, watch a television programme because there is a questionnaire for it, even though it is not a programme that person would ordinarily view at all. Here one problem of panels becomes clear: with all the best intentions, panel members may be considered to be specially interested in volunteering for, or accepting an invitation to join, a certain panel, and after a time the panel member can become rather too self-conscious and sophisticated. So it is necessary to change panel membership to stop conditioning from becoming too strong and this can add greatly to the cost of operating the panel. Nevertheless, with all their drawbacks, panels are interesting ways of collecting information and it is rather surprising that they have not been used more in academic research where ideas rather than pin-point accuracy of measurement may be the desired goal.

Focus groups

These groups are known by a variety of names, but the central idea is to bring together a small number of people who have certain interests or characteristics in common and to interview them as a group. Thus, for example, if one wanted to study the reactions of women readers of romantic novels to a change in the cover design of a series of books, a group of, say, eight women of varying ages and social classes could be got together either in a house or in a discussion room at a research agency and a trained discussion leader would ask questions of them about their reading interests and, generally speaking, what they expect romantic novels to look like. The participants clearly are *selected*, they cannot be random, and they must have some knowledge of the topic to be discussed. With a really good discussion leader the various members will all be drawn into the exchange of views and members can thus stimulate each other in a way that does not happen in individual interviews. However, it must be remembered that these groups work best at the initial stages of research when concepts still have to be clarified; they can never replace a properly constituted sample. The danger is that sometimes people who observe focus groups or read the reports on their discussions fall into the trap of saying that 'the majority' of members favoured a certain viewpoint, when this simply means five out of eight selected individuals. A focus group would be a most interesting way of beginning work on the previously noted research into why some people do and why some people do not go to the theatre, but the results of such discussion would be hypothesis-provoking only, not in any way hypothesis-testing.

Sampling in general

What has been said above about sampling can only hope to be the very lightest of scratches on the surface of what is a vast subject in itself. All that is intended here is that the would-be surveyor and sampler has some indication of the possibilities open in sampling methods and also a warning of the problems which sampling entails. There are a number of good books on sampling, some of them now particularly aimed at the social scientist, but even the best of books can only deal with problems in fairly general terms. Every survey which involves sampling has its own problems and the social researcher who can call on a statistician for advice should never fail to do so. There is nothing which can be guaranteed to alienate the affections of a statistician more than the surveyor who goes for advice after he has made a mess of sampling and needs someone to get him out of the mess.

THE INTERVIEW SCHEDULE

We now turn to consider what is involved in using the formal interview schedule for a properly constituted sample survey. After initial observations, perhaps participant observation, perhaps the use of focus groups and so on, the researcher worker may well end up carrying out a full social survey of a systematic kind. If the sampling procedure is all right, representative people from the sample will each be given standardized stimuli (questions) and their responses (answers) will be recorded in a pre-arranged manner. This means that the interview schedule itself has the function of a standardizing instrument. If the responses are to be analysed without a great deal of trouble it is probable that the likely answers have been thought of beforehand and that certain likely response categories are already incorporated in the schedule itself. Since the many responses will be presented in a statistical way (that is in tabular form) the well-designed schedule will be drafted with an eye to the presentation of the results in a clear and simple fashion. Very often one sees schedules which have never been taken beyond the question-asking stage and one wonders what terrible time and effort must be expended on forcing all sorts of answers into categories later on, especially when electronic means of analysis, such as computers, are to be used.

The interview schedule, then, is essentially an intermediate stage in research, and it fulfils a variety of functions. It enables a *team* of interviewers to give the same informants in the same predetermined order, and to record their responses in a standardized way. This also means that the interviewers are relieved of the problem of having to remember what questions are to be asked and, even more, the interviewer is relieved of having to enter the responses after the interview has ended, as in the case when no notes are taken, or only sketchy abbreviations of replies are made during the interview. The well drafted schedule only requires checking afterwards, it does not require another couple of hours' work trying to remember what people said or what one's own peculiar hieroglyphics made during the interview were meant to convey. In many cases the most probable answers can be set down in advance and this helps enormously towards analysis. One good way of judging a well-planned interview schedule of the formal type is to ask 'Could this schedule be handed over to someone else for analysis without them having to go back to the interviewer to ask what certain answers mean?' If the answer is 'no' then there must be ambiguities or inaccuracies in the recording of responses. In large-scale national surveys, as carried out regularly by market research firms and government agencies, interviews may be carried out over the whole country and the people who have the task of making the analysis of several hundred or thousand schedules cannot possibly be for ever phoning through to the interviewers to ask what some cryptic little scribble opposite question number 15 is supposed to mean.

Of course, not all the information written on interview

schedules will be by means of completely pre-determined answer categories. In some cases what are called open-ended questions will be asked and a verbatim reply may be recorded (if possible). But in many cases of recording factual information, opinions, attitudes and even physical characteristics (such as domestic facilities within a house), work done by the schedule designer before the questions are asked, or the observations made, can be repaid a dozen times over by the ease with which subsequent analysis can then be carried out.

From what has been said so far it is obvious that good interview schedules are important tools for the fieldworker. Many scientists spend weeks, or even months, in the construction of their own particular research apparatus. If the sociologist regards the interview schedule (and, as we shall discuss later, the questionnaire) in this way then he will not rush blithely into the field with a schedule which is the product of just a few hours' odd jottings on rough paper.

The design of schedules

In a book which was actually about statistics, A. L. Bowley once established four rules to guide designers of schedules and questionnaires.[3] They are given below as a starting point for our discussions. Bowley suggested that one should:

1 Ask for the minimum of information required.
2 Make sure that questions *can* be answered.
3 Make sure that questions *will* be answered truthfully.
4 Make sure that questions *will* be answered and not refused.

Point 1 made by Bowley is a more general and fundamental one than the other three and deserves special comment; it might be called the principle of parsimony. In many cases information can be gained from sources other than interviews. For example, in a closed institution, such as a factory, a school or a prison, the records will give a great deal of information about people who may be included in a survey. Why waste everyone's time asking questions which need not be asked when the information is already there? But also, the principle of parsimony should be used to keep the research down to essentials. There are always any number of questions which could be asked in a survey because they seem 'interesting'; but interest is not enough. A question, to be included, should be relevant to the problem being studied. If it is not relevant then it does not matter how 'interesting' it may be. This means that the schedule designer must always be asking himself why questions are being included in his schedule. If he can only argue to himself that they seem 'interesting' it is highly likely that he does not really know why he is putting them in, or what he will do with the answers when he gets them. Like Mr Micawber, he is hoping that 'something will turn up', and this is not the best way to run social surveys. Unfortunately in some ways, computers are capable of analysing and cross-tabulating vast amounts of data very quickly and this apparent ease of analysis seems to lead some people to extend their data collection. What must be remembered though is that whatever is asked and answered in a survey has to be inputted in some way and once it has been processed the output has to be read by someone. It is not therefore surprising that computing laboratories in universities put limits on the amount of output that users can expect in a given period of time. Self-indulgence, simply because facilities are there to be used, is a poor substitute for prior thought and it is amazing how much paper a few cross-tabulations can use up.

Bowley's other three points can be taken together since they cover various facets of the same main point – the questions themselves. To ask questions to which people cannot give answers is a waste of time for everyone – but one does, from time to time, come across schedules which include questions which require such feats of memory or such difficult calculations that no reasonable person can be expected to give an answer. To ask an ordinary person how many times they have visited the cinema during the past year is probably unfair for all except a small number who can quickly say 'never' or else 'regularly once a week without fail'. For other people it is probably impossible. To receive truthful answers from respondents is an expectation upon which all interviews are based. But truthfulness cannot be assumed in every instance. The very fact of suggesting things to people tends to result in inaccuracies. One market research survey into the purchase of a particular brand of ready-mix pudding named the article and asked housewives how often they bought it. The results totalled four times the actual sales over the period. In other cases we must be careful that questions will not result in refusals to answer. If this does happen the interviewer will have a rather embarrassing situation to overcome before going any further. Actual refusals to answer questions are always, in practice, fewer than might be expected. Surveys have been carried out quite successfully on such highly personal subjects as sexual behaviour and venereal diseases. Of course, some people will refuse to co-operate at all, but once an interview is under way most people will be prepared to answer questions so long as they seem genuine and relevant. But a survey on, let us say, political questions, which suddenly came up with questions about husband-wife relations, would almost certainly result in the questions being queried at the very least. It might be that the survey was aimed at testing a hypothesis that happily-married couples tend to vote more conservatively, while unhappily married couples vote more radically, but if this was not apparent to the informant the questions on marital relations would probably seem irrelevant and impertinent. All in all, then, the interview schedule must aim to ask a minimum of questions which can and will be answered. To do this it is best to work towards the final schedule in a systematic way.

Firstly, the basic hypotheses to be tested must be quite clear and these will immediately suggest the *topics* to be covered. These need not be anything more than the rough headings under which the detailed questions will fall. Once the topics are agreed, questions will be asked which will fill in the finer points of the hypotheses. It is almost certain that classificatory data on informants (e.g. sex, age, marital status, social class) will be relevant to subsequent analyses. The questions can be listed in rough under the headings (some people put each question on a card to begin with) and then they can be moved about so as to produce what seems to be a good 'flow' for the interview.

When this first draft has been done the researcher has something which can be worked on. If one knows *why* one is asking questions one will be able to see *how* one will produce the answers to the questions from the survey replies. Dummy blank tables can thus be drawn up before a single interview has even been carried out. The criterion of relevance is here quite crucial. Given that this work has been done, the draft schedule can then be examined in the closest detail – and probably torn to shreds.

Points of detail on schedule design

The questions that one asks in a survey must be derived from the object of the research itself: the schedule is only a tool for obtaining information. So there is no real point in framing questions before the broader areas of enquiry (the topics) have been decided on. Once the topics have been decided upon the questions will have a framework to fit into. For example, in a survey I carried out on the membership of the National Trust – one of the largest voluntary associations in Britain with over a million and a quarter members – it was decided that topics should include such things as how people came to join, how they felt about the payment of subscriptions, how much they read of the literature the Trust sent them, what their main interests in conservation were, how active a part they wanted to play in the work of the Trust, and so on. Once the topics had been set out in an order which would make sense to the recipients (in this case of a postal questionnaire) then the questions could be worked out.

When one is asking questions, however, one must never forget that the answers come from the respondents, so one must always be thinking about those respondents. Will they answer? Can they answer? Will they understand the point of this question? It is a very common feature in the first questions drafted by students in schedule designing to ask questions which patently have not been thought about from the respondents' point of view. The schedule designer must for every be putting himself or herself into the respondents' shoes and trying to imagine what it would be like to be asked this question by a stranger who just turned up a few minutes ago out of the blue. It is natural for a person who has been working towards a survey for several months to overlook the fact that the respondent has never heard of this wonderful enquiry and may be utterly baffled by it; but in this lies a great danger of asking poor questions, insufficiently considered from the respondents' viewpoint.

Many examples can be given of the pitfalls of question designing. One may use the term 'marital status' for analysis purposes, but to ask someone, 'What is your marital status?' migh result in some peculiar answers. Precision .is often needed if respondents are not to be confused; to ask a person about his or her 'family' could mean to a single man his parents and siblings, but to a married man his wife and children. In a survey of student activities one almost insuperable problem was to try to find out how many hours a week various sorts of students spent on 'practical work'. This term meant so many different things to different people that the results were almost impossible to classify. Technical words and jargon words are always potential dangers, but ambiguities in questions are probably even more dangerous. There is a story of a market research interviewer who was questioning a person about ready-sliced cheese. The informant was asked when she last ate a cheese slice and then the question was put 'And what did you have it on?' Back came the answer, 'The settee'.

We will discuss problems such as these in chapter 8 by

using an actual schedule which incorporates examples of mistakes, but before doing this we must also consider the problems which arise from lack of understanding of the question. In a survey on shopping which I made a few years ago one of my student interviewers was questioning an old lady about the grocer's shop she used. The survey was a comparison between self-service and counter-service grocers and the student was puzzled that the old lady claimed to shop at a counter-service yet all her answers suggested that she used a self-service shop. In the end the student asked the lady if she really did mean that her grocer was a counter-service shop and the old lady replied, 'Oh yes, it's counter-service all right. All the things are out on counters and you go round helping yourself.' Fortunately this was in a pilot survey and the warning was heeded in the survey proper.

One difficulty about questioning is that of leading the respondent towards a particular response. If people are asked 'Would you like . . .', there is a good chance that they will say 'yes'. Although the question may seem clumsier for it, it is absolutely necessary to give a genuine choice, and even though it may sound stilted to ask, 'Do you approve or disapprove of . . .', at least this presents a fair choice. For examples of carefully worded questions in public opinion polls it is worth looking at the newspapers to see how very carefully the professional market research firms word their questions when they are asking ordinary people for their current political views. The phraseology may at times seem a little stilted but this is necessary to avoid misleading people.

A further regular pitfall in framing questions is the double question. This is very often to be spotted by the word 'and' linking two separate items. For example the question 'Would you like to become a doctor and work in a hospital?' is a double question because the respondent might like to become a doctor, but not work in a hospital. This is an obvious example, but more subtle ones crop up frequently and they indicate that the designer has thought only of asking the question, not of trying to answer it.

A great deal of faulty question phrasing stems from survey workers being over-involved in their own ideas. Often the survey is to be conducted after months of work on a theme, and by this time the researcher has become immersed in the work and tends to forget that other people do not have the same interest or knowledge. For reasons such as this it is important to ensure that the 'final edition' of the interview schedule has been adequately gone over and tried out before it is used in the full-scale field survey. I suggest there there are a number of steps which should be gone through towards this end.

Testing of interview schedules

The important fact about a field survey is that it is a once-and-for-all operation which cannot be repeated. It is no use realizing at the analysis stage that question 3 is ambiguous and all the respondents should be asked it again in a different way. I doubt if any survey has ever been carried out without the researcher having some regrets at the analysis stage about some questions which could have been phrased better, but the good researcher makes sure in advance that these regrets are as few as possible. I suggest that the regrets can be kept to a minimum by using the following steps:

1 pre-pilot open interviews;
2 roughing-out questions and layout;
3 internal testing;
4 pilot survey;
5 survey proper.

These five steps are a counsel of perfection, but most surveys can include them to some degree. The pre-pilot open interviews will be conducted with a small sub-sample of the population concerned and will, in the earliest stages, be as much hypothesis-seeking as anything else. But this stage is vitally important for the researcher to get the feel of the situation. In many instances of social research the research workers are going to survey a group of people who are quite different from themselves. They may be working among old people, or schoolchildren, or even convicts. To start framing questions without first having talked to some of the people concerned about one's ideas would be ludicrous.

Having carried out such interviews (and no set limit to them can be laid down) researchers may then make a start on their topic headings and detailed questions. It is virtually certain that they will require details of the personal characteristics of the informants, in many cases such facts as sex, age, marital status, social class, educational level, and so on. These details are often called 'classificatory data' since they are frequently used for the classification of other questions. For example, distinctions often need to be made between the opinions of men and women, single people and married people, young people and old people. Classificatory data provide one side of the subsequent table for analysis purposes. Even at an early stage in the enquiry it may well be possible to decide what actual classifications will be used for these data. Male and female classification is simple. 'Single', 'married', 'widowed' and 'any other' will probably suffice for marital status unless the survey is particularly concerned with divorced or legally separated people. Social class may well be based on the occupation of the male head of the household according to a pre-determined scale, such as, in Britain, that of the Registrar-General, or the Market Research Society. There may be problems of deciding the social class of married women, but these will have to be settled at some time. Educational level will probably be analysed by the last educational institution attended full-time in some hierarchical fashion, or by the actual educational attainments of the informant.

Age may be classified according to any set of categories deemed useful for the purpose in hand. Obviously, five-year categories will be more discriminating, but they may be unnecessarily small grades. A ten-year age-group is more likely to be useful, but the actual category limits should be carefully thought about. It may be attractive to use 20-29 as a category, but if there is any importance in the study attached to distinguishing between adults and minors obviously 18 must be a cut-off point. There might be more advantage in making the categories run mid-way across the ten-year groups, giving 25-34 as a group if it is felt that some significant changes take place in people's lives in their mid-thirties, or at other points in the mid-sections of the decades. This classification certainly helps by creating a category beginning at 65, the usual age of retirement for men. Obviously all age-groups are arbitrary; the point being made here is that the actual divisions used should be chosen for their usefulness in classifying people for the purposes of the research being undertaken, and this decision should be considered at an early stage.

The topics themselves will probably be reasonably apparent after the pre-pilot interview stage and two decisions need to be made at the layout stage. First, what order should the topics be in, and second, what questions should be asked under each topic heading? Let us suppose that the survey is concerned with leisure activities and is a comparison between social classes. Obviously the classificatory data will give special attention to the factor of social class and also to such important variables as age, sex, marital status, and so on. The topic headings might then discriminate between leisure activities within the home – individual and collective; leisure activities outside the home – organized and unorganized; and use of commercial leisure facilities. These five possible areas of leisure activities are only illustrative for the particular methodological problem here being discussed; they are not in fact derived from any research, but they will suffice to show that the researcher should now be thinking in what order they might be placed so as to give a sensible progression in an interview. It might well be that the researcher decided to start inside the home with individual activities, and lead on to collective ones. Then he or she might move to outside the home, taking unorganized ones before organized ones, and then conclude with commercial leisure. The point here is that the order of topics would then, we hope, seem sensible *to the informant*. It is very important indeed that the informant be considered at the earliest possible stage since he or she will be doing the work of supplying answers to the questions and a good 'flow' in the interview will help greatly in establishing and maintaining interest and rapport.

The questions themselves can then be fitted in under the topic headings decided upon. Some people like to use a card for each question at this stage so that it is simple to move questions about as it seems desirable to order and re-order them in the best sequence. At this stage the actual response categories may not have been considered in detail, but if the questions themselves justify inclusion some thought should have been given to the response categories envisaged for analysis since it is the *answers* which will be analysed. Nevertheless, the questions themselves, at this stage, will be the main focus, and also at this stage we might allow more questions to be included than are likely to be used at the final stage. When they are all put together under topic headings the full interview schedule will then tell us how long the interview is likely to take and if it is much too long some pruning can be undertaken at once. The writing stage, when topics and questions are actually put down, can be quite a salutary experience. What seemed to be a simple matter when merely held as a mental question, verbally unframed and with no thought given to response, appears as a simply impossible problem when it has actually to be put down on paper. We may, for example, think to ourselves that it would be very useful to ask a housewife if she works outside the house at all, and this sounds easy enough in our heads. But as soon as we have to commit this question to paper we discover (or we certainly *should* discover) that this is a difficult question to ask with absolute clarity. There seems to be no end to the possible replies we could receive and the job of categorizing them seems a nightmare.

At this stage we are only roughing-out our interview schedule, but the more attention we can give to detail now the more we are likely to be saving ourselves trouble later on. Decisions to postpone the actual wording or analysis categories can often be rationalized as being safeguards against too rigid a mental outlook on what may be a very exploratory field of research. But there are numerous instances which come to my mind of research in which all the problems of analysis were left until the survey had been done and then anything up to, or even over, a year was needed to sort out the tangled mass of answers to vague questions. Much of this sort of work is unnecessary if forethought is used at the planning stage.

When a draft schedule has been produced the next stage is what I have referred to previously as 'internal testing'. This means trying the schedule out, *not* on a sample of people for whom it is intended in its final version, but on people who may well be one's colleagues at work; that is, people who are likely to know something about survey work itself and schedule design. The point of this stage is that it is cheap and easy, and does not necessitate going outside the building. But the results can be absolutely invaluable if one's colleagues look over the draft and, with no holds barred, pick on every doubtful point. I recall some years ago that a young postgraduate student who was designing a schedule containing a lot of attitude questions had his schedule internally tested at this stage by a number of people and practically every question he had put was a double one. Had he gone out with the schedule the results would have been chaotic, yet he himself had not seen these double questions until they were pointed out to him at the internal testing stage. Probably the most valuable thing about this stage is that the schedule compiler gets a sort of 'consumers' view' for the first time. A commonplace fault among schedule designers, as mentioned earlier, is not thinking enough about what it is like to be on the receiving end of the questions. If one is brave enough to try the draft out on critical, expert colleagues, one can be reasonably sure that what emerges at the end will be free of double questions, ambiguities, leading questions, and so on, and the helpful colleagues, in pretending to be informants, will also probably have thought up some difficult-to-classify answers too. All in all, this is a valuable stage which researchers who do not accept criticism very easily will probably wish to avoid, but if they do consciously and deliberately avoid it, they have only themselves to blame for not taking advantage of a most useful and quite inexpensive step in schedule preparation.

After the mauling received from his dear colleagues, the designer eventually produces what he hopes will be a document which meets the internal criticisms. It next goes to a small sample of the real consumers for testing. This is the 'dress rehearsal' or pilot stage.

Views on the function of the pilot stage vary among research workers, but I view the pilot stage as being the last one before the actual survey itself and therefore the stage where, as far as possible, the interview schedule is as near to its final form in both questions and answer categories as it can be. I see little value in the interview schedule going into the field to a small sub-sample of respondents if the designer knows in advance that there is a lot of work still to be done. If this work is apparent it seems only sensible to do it and *then* try out as good a schedule as one can produce on the real people. After all, the survey will have to be done at some stage and it is only going to be helpful to carry out a pilot if it tells the designer something he did not know. There is little to be gained in trying out something which one already knows to be inadequate. In my view the importance of the pilot stage is that it confronts the perhaps over-sophisticated schedule with down-to-earth respondents. By this I mean that both the designer and colleagues may be *too* expert, too sophisticated, too used to jargon, too well-educated and able to verbalize. And, in addition, they will all understand the purpose of the survey. The respondents, in a normal population, will contain much larger numbers of unsophisticated, poorly educated, inarticulate and non-jargon-using people whose task it will be to try to answer questions, some of which may be quite baffling to them. The pilot survey should be the crucial stage at which the surveyor is forced to come down from the ivory tower and communicate with the respondents. It is at the pilot stage that 'stuffiness' in the wording of questions becomes very apparent. Questions may look all right on paper simply because we accept a more formal style in writing than we do in speech, but they may sound absolutely frightful when put into speech. A simple example will suffice: many people when writing use the word 'commence' rather than 'begin'. In a written question it would be possible to ask, 'In what year did you commence secondary education?' Just try saying that sentence out loud and see how pompous and unnatural it sounds. A further small point: we may have been taught at school to avoid ending written sentences with a preposition, but the above sentence, apart from replacing 'commence' by 'begin', *sounds* more natural if we do in fact end it with the preposition. Try saying out loud, 'what year did you begin your secondary education in?' This, surely, is much more like what we really would say in a normal conversation.

One further point about the pilot stage is its value in helping in problems of analysis. The response categories are just as important as the questions at this stage, and even a relatively small number of real-life responses can help in re-drafting response categories. We may find that a particular reply which we had expected to be only given very occasionally looks as if it might well be much more prevalent than we had expected. We might, for example, find that in a particular residential area there are unexpectedly large numbers of households with 'lodgers' and so we might want to add this as a specific category in the household composition; or we might find that on an attitude question views are rather more extreme than we had anticipated and so a new response category could be usefully put in to save us noting responses under 'Others, specify . . .' in many cases.

When the lessons from the pilot survey have been fully learned alterations can be made where necessary, but if the work done prior to the pilot has been adequate the alterations consequent upon it should not be great. Indeed, it could be regarded as a measure of the previous work how little needs doing after the pilot. But when all has been considered the next and final step is the survey itself. This involves a number of considerations and these will be dealt with under separate headings. Perhaps the most general point to be made about the survey proper is that it should be regarded as an end-point to be reached after careful preparation. Whatever mistakes are made in the survey will be irrevocable. A poor response rate cannot be botched over. A badly-phrased question cannot be re-worded after the survey is complete. Everything that can be done in preparation for the survey should therefore be done; there is precious little that can be done afterwards without distorting the accuracy of the survey. Alterations made afterwards have a tendency to show; those which do not show may be examples of dishonesty by the surveyor.

Surveys vary enormously in their nature according to the purpose of the enquiry and the sample of informants approaced. The problems encountered in a survey of the occupants of old people's homes will obviously be different from those encountered in trying to interview a representative sample of ordinary adolescents. We are not here concerned with the problems involved in obtaining samples; our focus is on the survey once the sample has been decided on and drawn. For the sake of convenience in discussing problems of surveying we will use the ordinary house-to-house survey as the general case for discussion.

CONTACTING INFORMANTS

One of the basic problems in surveying is to obtain a good response from one's informants. When we discuss the use of self-completed questionnaires this will be a special point of detail, but it can be a major problem in interview surveys also. In a survey of a 'closed' institution such as a prison or a firm the informants may be instructed to co-operate with interviewers because of agreement about the survey by the people in authority, but in many instances of samples from the general population no such authority exists and surveyors must try to obtain co-operation as best they can by interesting the informants in the survey and gaining their completely free co-operation. What is surprising is how very generously this co-operation is given in many cases. Market research firms, government research agencies, academic research units and many other organizations which carry out survey interviews depend for their success on the voluntary help given to them by members of the general public. A great deal of interviewing is done by approaching people in the street or by knocking on people's doors. It is fairly rare these days to find adults who have never been interviewed in any survey. Not very long ago I found myself being interviewed in a university survey on residential mobility in which some of my own students were fieldworkers. I have also been interviewed on trains and on a cross-channel ferry about my travel habits. In recent years interviews by telephone have become popular with some commerical research firms, but to some respondents this approach must seem rather intrusive and slightly dubious in that there is no way of properly checking the credentials of the telephone caller. Clearly, the telephone interview is attractively cheap, but in my opinion it is also a technique which could well irritate the respondents approached.

Personal approach

Let us consider what the interviewer is trying to do when seeking an interview and what the reaction of the informant may be. The interviewer is seeking to interview a sample of housewives on an estate about, let us say, the work-day pattern of wives who work only within the home. The sample has been based on a random choice of houses. The interviewer wants (a) to find out if the informant is a full-time housewife and (b) if so, how she spends her working day. If the woman says 'yes' to (a) the interviewer wants to ask her a whole list of questions about her life. On the other hand, the housewife, engaged in her working day, hears a knock on the door and finds a complete stranger there with a clip-board to which is attached a rather large sheet (or sheets) of paper covered with duplicated sentences and ominous boxes. Let us try to consider, from both sides, what is needed to move from this initial confrontation to a successfully completed interview.

The interviewer (let us say it is a man for ease of being able to say 'he' and 'she' in this case, even though most interviewers are women) will expect to open the conversation and he has the task of explaining to the housewife, simply and briefly:

1 where he is from (the sponsoring body);
2 what he is doing (the purpose of the survey);
3 why the housewife was chosen in the sample;
4 why she should grant the interview.

Looking at it from the housewife's point of view her phrasing of these questions would be:

1 Who are you and where are you from?
2 What do you want?
3 Why choose me to help you?
4 Why should I help you anyway?

If dealt with in this order the opening gambit would be (1) 'I am an interviewer from the North Midlands Institute for Social Research and (2) we are carrying out a survey of the working-day of housewives. (3) Your house has come up in a random sample of houses in this area and, if you are a full-time housewife, we would like you to tell us about your working day since (4) we believe that a survey of this subject would be of great value in helping all housewives.'

In the above passage points (1) and (2) are easier to explain than points (3) and (4). Point (3), on sampling, is a technical matter which is very difficult to explain properly and it might well be beyond the abilities of many housewives to understand without more explanation what random sampling means. But fortunately most people who are asked to help in surveys are prepared to accept that they are appropriate people to answer questions on the survey for which they are approached, and particularly where people feel that they are being asked to give 'expert' information this can be seen as rather a compliment: 'If you want to know about how a housewife organizes her day *I* can tell you everything you need to know.' But while people in the sample *can* give the information, the question still has to be answered as to *why* they should bother. In most cases the reasonable answer will be along the lines that those people who give information for the survey will be contributing to an overall study, the results of which will be useful for a better understanding by everyone of the general problem and will also particularly help specialists who might be interested in (in this case) the housewife's day. These specialists might be architects, furniture manufacturers, social workers, magazine publishers, domestic equipment manufacturers, shopkeepers – all the people who are affected by the housewife's day. The fictitious example being used here is not the easiest one to explain to an informant, but many much more difficult ones have been explained and interviews obtained.

Approach by letter

One possible way of getting round the problem of the 'doorstep' explanation is to write a letter to people in the sample to let them know in advance of the survey and the coming call by an interviewer. One advantage of a letter is that all the points (1) to (4) can be dealt with in advance and so the interviewer is expected and time is saved in not having to go through all the verbal explanations. In some cases, especially among people of higher status, the letter is regarded as a more polite way of asking for the interview and it helps differentiate the interviewer, when he or she calls, from marauding salesmen. Against the use of a letter it must be noted that it is not easy to write a short but very clear letter explaining everything the informant may want to know, and if the recipient decides that she or he does not want to co-operate then she/he is warned in advance of the interviewer's call. If she is determined not to be interviewed she could even write back and say quite clearly 'keep away', in which case no earnest explanation by the interviewer is possible. Ther is also the danger with sending a letter that people may misread it — or just look at it and not read it properly. I have myself been welcomed as a local council surveyor come to look at houses in a slum area, and I had an assistant who was once received as a person who was trying to recruit voluntary social workers. These instances arose because the recipients just did not read the letters sent to them.

However, sending a letter to a large sample of people can be quite a costly business, not only in stationery and postage, but also in finding out the recipients' correct names and addresses, if one is to avoid the very impersonal and rather off-putting form of address, 'The Occupant'. For these reasons alone many surveyors decide not to send letters in advance and rely on the interviewers' skills in being able to explain to people on their doorsteps what the survey is about and why they should help with it.

THE INTERVIEW AND THE INTERVIEWER

The qualities required of interviewers will vary greatly according to the complexities of interview schedules used and also the degree of informality permitted in the interviews. In academic, exploratory research where the results are not to be analysed and presented in statistical fashion a research worker may feel that he or she cannot have an assistant to help with interviews since the whole approach is very subjective and non-statistical. But where results can be presented in tabular form it does seem reasonable to expect that there is sufficient uniformity of approach to have allowed for more than one interviewer, and, of course, for subsequent repetition of the interviews, so as to replicate the enquiry. Wherever there appears to be a 'mystique' about the interviewing — suggestions that these results were possible because of some mystical skills possessed by the interviewer — then one is likely to be moving from social science towards journalism, or special pleading at the very least. Interviewing is certainly a skilled job when carried out properly, but it is not a mystical union between interviewer and respondent. Obviously some people make better interviewers than others, but with training no normal person who is reasonably able to carry on a conversation should find it impossible to undertake interviews. Hundreds of ordinary men and women are highly competent interviewers, and a glance at some of the very complex interview schedules used by market research firms and the government research agencies show that they are capable of carrying out very intricate interviews which would probably be beyond the capabilities of many untrained academics!

The ideal schedule is one which can be used by a team of interviewers and yield the same stimuli to informants with their responses being recorded in the same way. The survey interview therefore requires expertise, not 'flair', on the interviewer's part. This does not mean that the interviewer becomes a cold clinical robot, but it does mean that he or she uses a particular instrument in the way that it is designed to be used – for objective study. The interviewer who changes questions, who adds bits to questions, who generally messes about with the schedule, is not being clever, he/she is being a bad fieldworker.

All interviewers should be carefully briefed on the schedule they are about to use, and wherever possible a 'guide to interviewers' should accompany, or be incorporated with, the schedule. Where interviewers are centrally grouped they can be called together for a briefing session, when any queries can be raised and dealt with on the spot, but where large organizations have interviewers scattered about the country this may be a counsel of perfection, although peripatetic fieldwork supervisors do invaluable work in this as well as other areas.

Interviewers must seek out, contact and interview their allotted sub-samples, and once they have been given their tasks they must work relatively independently. In the case of street interviews, where they may be working on 'quota' samples (so many people of certain sex, age and class categories chosen by the interviewer to fit into the required quota), the discretion allowed may be considerable. The temptation to 'fiddle' quotas or interviews is always present, and for an interviewer who is not getting interviews this temptation must at times be great. Nevertheless, the whole basis of survey work is one of trust and relatively few interviewers abuse this trust. It is important that fieldwork should be properly supervised and that is why all professional research agencies get their field supervisors to make check calls on people who have been included in a sample and why fieldworkers should always have someone to turn to if they have any doubts or are in any difficulties. In my own survey of visitors to the British Museum in which teams of five interviewers worked for four separate weeks interviewing at the museum entrances I made sure that I was present for at least the first day of each survey and was available by phone during the rest of the time. The first day of each survey was crucial in sorting out minor problems for the interviewers which only came to be recognized once the fieldwork was under way.

After interviews have been conducted, interviewers must check their schedules for errors of recording, omissions, or any other faults, and good supervision will again ensure that this is done. The ultimate aim of interviewers is to produce a well-completed schedule for every interview assigned to them. The ability to win over an informant who is undecided whether or not to grant the interview is important, as is the ability to put people at their ease and reassure them that the interview is not going to be some sort of *viva voce* examination. These are the human skills of the interviewer which will obtain good interviews without over-assisting the informants. At the end of an interview the informant will be thanked for co-operating and left feeling satisfied after what was an interesting and worthwhile discussion. But apart from having the quality of tact, the interviewer will also have the quality of accuracy, since the results of the interviews, on the schedules, will go to other people — office staff — whose task will be the analysis.

Before considering the problems of analysis we will next make a parallel study of the problems involved in the use of self-completed questionnaires. When this has been done the common problems of analysis can be dealt with.

7

The Self-completed Questionnaire

INTRODUCTION

In contrast to the interview schedule, which is used by the interviewer as an *aide-mémoire* and which is completed by the interviewer, the questionnaire is normally completed without a research worker being present at all; the informant has written instructions before him and fills in the questionnaire himself. This description of the questionnaire is, however, a generalized one, and questionnaires vary quite a lot in the way they are administered. Perhaps the best-known example of a questionnaire sent by post is the income tax form, which all tax payers receive each year, requiring complete details to be given of income and certain expenditure. Another famous questionnaire is the one used in the decennial census of population. In Britain this quesionnaire is delivered to each dwelling by a census officer (usually a local government official) and collected by the same officer a few days later. While the census questionnaire contains an enormous number of helpful instructions for its completion, the census officer may also give help to respondents if they are still baffled by it. Some questionnaires may be distributed to a particular group of people who are together in a particular place. I have myself designed a questionnaire which was used for the study of church congregations. The questionnaires were handed out during the service and the clergyman explained the purpose of the survey and gave people verbal guidance, instead of giving a sermon. I also pioneered work on surveys of theatre audiences using self-completed questionnaires handed to people as they entered the auditorium.[1] In these surveys research assistants handed out pencils to help people fill in the answers and collected completed questionnaires from them either before the performance began or during an interval. This technique produced very high response rates. A rather more unusual self-completed questionnaire was used alongside the interviews already mentioned in the British Museum visitors's survey. It was recognized before the survey began that there would be some overseas visitors who could not be interviewed in English so a short (one-page), basic self-completion questionnaire was drafted and printed in French, German, Spanish and Japanese. In each survey this added between 7 and 8 per cent to the total of visitors who were respondents and left only a handful of people who were non-respondents because of language difficulties. The self-completed questionnaire is a reasonably flexible means of collecting information if used with a little imagination. I can recall filling in a travel questionnaire for QANTAS airlines a few years ago on the way to Australia and being quite grateful to them for giving me something interesting to do on a long, boring flight.

For the purposes of this chapter, however, we will concentrate on the questionnaire which is circulated through the post, since this is a very commonplace use of this particular technique for collecting information. The problems arising from it will be considered under two headings — the respondents and the information to be collected.

THE RESPONDENTS

One of the great attractions of the postal questionnaire enquiry is its apparent ease and cheapness. Rather than having to spend many hours, at high cost, sending out interviewers

armed with interview schedules to locate and talk to informants, all one need do is knock out a list of questions, have
them duplicated, put the whole lot in an envelope addressed
to the informant (with a stamped self-addressed envelope
enclosed) and then sit back while the Post Office and the
recipients do all the work. In theory this sounds so delightful
that it is surprising anyone considers interviews worth bothering with at all. In fact, with the increasing popularity of
sociology and quasi-sociology, it is unfortunately true that
far too many questionnaires are sent out these days. Voluntary
organizations — some of good repute, but others of little
standing in the community — have been caught in the thralls
of this new game, and even official research bodies themselves
seem now to have the questionnaire bug and to produce
what are probably the longest and most complicated questionnaires of the lot. One university librarian told me recently
that he now receives so many questionnaires that he is
rapidly becoming fed up with them and is considering refusing
to co-operate on any of them in the future.[2]

There are various reasons for the popularity of questionnaires as research tools. First, as was said, they seem to be a
very cheap way of collecting data, especially when compared
with the undoubted expense of interviews. Paper still costs
relatively little and even with increasing postal charges a
hundred or two questionnaires do not make much of a hole
in a research grant. Perhaps an even greater attraction to the
researcher is that so much of the work *seems* to be done for
you by the respondents. It is also possible, for a relatively
small fee and a very small addition to the standard postal rate
in Britain, to use specially printed business reply envelopes
whereby the recipient pays only for those envelopes he
receives back. This, again, may seem very attractive since it
can save the researcher from wasting money if the recipient
is a non-respondent. All in all, the self-completion postal
questionnaire seems, prima facie, to be a most attractive way
of carrying out a survey, producing large amounts of data at
minimal trouble and cost.

But not even the Garden of Eden was without its problems and the big snag to postal questionnaires is that of non-response. Too often, especially in newspaper reports, one reads of the numbers of questionnaires that a survey has been based upon, but one is not always told what proportion of replies was achieved. So, although it may sound reasonably impressive to read that a survey is based on, let us say, 750 respondents, it is much less impressive if we know that this was from a total sample of 2,500 questionnaires sent out. If the report says, therefore, that two-thirds of respondents were in favour of some policy or reform, this means 500 out of 750 *respondents*. But 500 respondents out of a total sample of 2,500 is only one-fifth, which is much less impressive. The real truth about the total response to the question discussed is that out of 2,500 people asked 20 per cent were in favour, 10 per cent were opposed and 70 per cent expressed no view at all because they did not reply. Of course it is unrealistic to hope for a 100 per cent response to any survey, however it is conducted, but in questionnaires especially there is a particular danger of people playing a simple numbers game and hoping to impress when they should really be playing a proportions game.

Non-response, then, is one of the greatest problems in postal questionnaire surveys, and it is necessary to consider it from a number of angles. First, we will consider why postal surveys should be useful, second, for what sort of respondents they are particularly useful, and third, what can be done to get a maximum response from them.

Suppose that we were trying to find out how people spend their leisure time, and a general sample of all sorts of people was desirable. To send out a questionnaire to people of all ages and classes might seem reasonable at first glance, but our hopes of a good response would probably be dashed by non-response. First, many people will not be in the slightest bit interested in our survey, and, not having the persuasive interviewer there to tell them why the survey is so important, they will just throw the questionnaire away. These people could complete it, but in fact they will not. Second, some people unused to receiving postal enquiries of this sort will feel that this is all too complicated for them; they will not be able to understand why the survey is being done, or how the answers should be given, so they also will throw it away. These people might respond verbally to an interviewer, but the written document is beyond them.

The 'cannots' will include the illiterates and the near-illiterates of our society, and thus a section of the lower intelligence levels will be cut out, resulting in some bias towards the higher intelligence levels. But the 'will nots' are likely to be just as important in the non-response, since they are the people who just don't see why they should give their time and energy to filling in these damn fool question-naires that have just landed out of the blue on the breakfast table from some organization they have never heard of in their lives. People with a wide range of interests, who take a lively interest in the society in which they live, may be expected to be favourably predisposed to filling in question-naires, but how many people can we expect to find in this category? And how representative are they anyway of the general mass of the population? It therefore looks as if a general sample would give us a response biased towards livelier, more literate, more intelligent people. We should also expect, a priori, that we would get a better response from people who did already have an interest in the subject of our enquiry. Mothers of small children living in the area of a criminal lunatic asylum might well be more favourably dis-posed to answering a questionnaire on attitudes to the treatment of criminals than women who have never had children who live in an area where there are no prisons within miles. Interest, particularly self-interest, is a factor conducive towards completing questionnaires. It is therefore useful to give special consideration to the questionnaire as a tool for surveying particular groups of people who may be assumed to have a personal interest in the subject of the enquiry.

A questionnaire sent to members of a professional association from their own headquarters on a matter of vital interest to them all should obtain a good response, particularly if the topic is one on which there are fairly strong views on opposing sides. A questionnaire enquiry sent to people who are themselves involved in a matter under survey should gain a good response. An enquiry about the reasons for withdrawal from employment among women teachers is of both importance and interest to the women involved. In this instance, which was actually studied by R.K. Kelsall, a very high response rate of 84 per cent was achieved.[3]

A further point may suggest itself from some of the examples given above. Although it might, for some questions, be desirable to interview women teachers, they are a group who are not all to be found conveniently located in one area of the country. Indeed, for any particular goup of women teachers trained at a particular time a certain proportion are quite likely to have left this country altogether. The postal questionnaire (so long as addresses can be traced) enables the surveyor to get in touch with the sample no matter where they may be, so long as postal services can reach them. Part of the women teachers' enquiry was devoted to tracing respondents by sending lists of names to women trained together and asking if they still had contact with each other. Tracing the current location of sample members can be a very intricate and frustrating process, but once this is done the respondents can be contacted anywhere in the world.

Looking at the question of the respondents, then, it is clear that the postal questionnaire enquiry is particularly well suited to special groups of people who are likely to be widely dispersed geographically. In my own surveys of members of the National Trust, who are obviously scattered all over the United Kingdom, a postal questionnaire was the only possible way to sample any significant number of members with the very limited financial resources I had available. Fortunately, Trust members tend to be well-educated, interested people, so the response rate was good.[4]

THE INFORMATION

Many years ago Sidney and Beatrice Webb gave a good example of how *not* to construct a questionnaire in their *Methods of Social Study*. A questionnaire they devised for sending to trade unions would probably have taken a dozen people a dozen years to complete, if they could indeed have managed to complete it at all. No questionnaire which is daunting to the recipient is likely to produce much enthusiasm, and while interviewees may be carried along by the social relationships established in the talk of an interview, the questionnaire respondent who looks through 20 pages of closely printed questions alone is hardly to be expected to thrill in anticipation. No questionnaire which is too long and involved can be expected to have a favourable reception, and the limitations of the questionnaire method must be accepted. In the interview a particular topic can be made the focus of a number of questions without seeming to be too prying so long as the informant is interested in the topic itself. But if a questionnaire attempts the same amount of 'probing' (to use the technical term) it is likely to look both over-complicated and probably too inquisitorial. A skilled interviewer can cope with a large number of often personal questions and be guided by instructions as to which questions to follow on with if particular answers are given, and which questions to drop in other cases. The respondent in the well-conducted interview is made to feel that this is all very simple because of the skill of the interviewer. With a questionnaire, however, the skill is in the layout of the questionnaire itself, and in the recipient, as to how well he or she can understand the questions. The difference is a very important one indeed and has fundamental effects on the limits of the questionnaire.

As a general principle, the interview is likely to be most suitable for questions seeking 'depth', while the questionnaire (particularly on large samples) is likely to get 'breadth' of coverage on reasonably straightforward questions. To assist the respondent in completing a questionnaire — and this should always be one of the questionnaire designer's prime aims — given answers are helpful. It is simpler to tick a box, or ring a word or phrase than it is to write in one's own answer, and this is likely to make for easier analysis too. But including given answers takes up space on the questionnaire, so that a balance must be held. The whole problem of questionnaire enquiries is how far one can go with the questions and how much one can anticipate the reactions of the respondents. What looks to the designer to be a useful set of alternative responses, all there to help the respondent, may look to the respondent to be a daunting set of complicated phrases and boxes. What may be thought to be a help may in fact be a hindrance, and it must always be remembered that for better or worse (and it may well be for worse), the respondent sees the whole of the questionnaire at one go. There is no way of feeding questions one by one as in an interview. If he or she is put off by the size or appearance of the questionnaire that partcular respondent is lost to the survey. He or she may also, of course, go a certain way with the answers and then decide enough is enough, a situation which rarely occurs in an interview. It is clear that if one is to get a response the recipient must be made to feel that the whole business is worthwhile, and for this the instructions and appeal which precede the questions themselves are of paramount importance. We will call this section the 'covering letter' since it is, so often, written in the form of a letter from the surveyor.

THE COVERING LETTER

While an interviewee can initially be approached by letter and the letter followed up with the actual interview, such a separation is hardly feasible for a postal questionnaire enquiry. In this case the introduction and the collection of the information must be done together, and the introduction must cover many of the matters dealt with by the interviewer in initiating the interview. These matters may be considered as ways of dealing with possible questions raised by the recipient.

What is this circular letter and set of questions about? The covering letter must, very quickly and simply, tell the recipient *who* is carrying out the survey and *what* is being surveyed. Fancy jargon and long words will not help here. A direct and simple explanation is needed.

Why is this survey being carried out? Here a reasonable explanation of the value of the survey is necessary to convince the recipient that this is a job worth helping with. If the survey can clearly be related to some burning issue of the day, all the better.

Why ask me to help you? Here some very brief explanation of how the recipient came to be included in the sample is required. Since some form of random sampling has probably been used this part can be used to stress the need for a good response rate.

Why should *I* give my time to answering all these questions? To answer this the surveyor can point out that if all the recipients reply they will be contributing information and views which, when analysed, will be of value for whatever group or institution is relevant.

What will happen to my questionnaire if I do fill it in? This question requires a guarantee of anonymity and an assurance that all questionnaires will eventually be destroyed after analysis.

It can be seen that a covering letter which deals simply, clearly and *briefly* with the above points must be carefully constructed. A further point which is very relevant is that the recipient must be absolutely clear about who the survey is being carried out by. Headed notepaper is customarily used by research organizations, and it is sensible and courteous for the covering letter to be signed wherever possible and to have below the signature the typed name of the signator and the status he or she holds in the organization. Not only does this make the appeal seem more personal, but is also gives the recipient a real person to write to if there are any queries to raise about the survey. If the letter is separate from the acual questionnaire itself the recipient can retain it after returning the completed questionnaire and thus has some tangible record of the event. It is a matter for the researcher's judgement as to whether an appeal letter signed by oneself is always the best tactfic. In the case of the National Trust surveys I used covering letters over the signature of the Secretary in one case and the Director-General in another. For a survey of undergraduates and their use of books at Sheffield University the appeal letter went out over the signature of the chairman of the library committee. In all these cases it was made clear to recipients that I was carrying out the research, but the 'sponsorship' of the signatories was felt to help in stressing the co-operation between research and administrator.

FACILITATING REPLIES

A good covering letter is obviously very important in questionnaire work. But other things can be done to help get a good response rate.

It is grossly impertinent to send a questionnaire by post and to expect the recipient to pay the return postage. Some even worse cases do occur, where the recipient does not even receive an addressed envelope; in these cases the sender does not deserve to get a single reply. When people are asked to fill in questionnaires they are being asked to give time and quite often a fair amount of mental energy for a task which will benefit them personally very little, and the end product of which they may never see. I must be appreciated, then, that the respondents are doing a great favour to the researcher, and they must not be expected to incur one penny in costs in doing this. It is therefore essential that questionnaires be accompanied by postage-paid, addressed envelopes which will be used for the return of the completed questionnaire.

It is possible to save money in Britain on large-scale postal surveys by using the Business Reply Service operated by the Post Office. This service, and the similar 'Freepost' service, is used a great deal by commerical advertisers and may therefore be thought to be slightly suspect for survey work. At one time I used to be strongly in favour of using actual postage stamps for non-commercial social surveys on the grounds that the provision of a reply envelope with a genuine stamp on it indicated a genuine expectation of a reply. However, in recent years I have been involved in postal surveys with samples of up to six and seven thousand and in these cases the use of stamped reply envelopes was out of the question, so business reply envelopes were used. With these very large numbers and respondents who could be expected to take a favourable view of replying I do not think that the business reply service greatly reduced the response. With much smaller postal questionnaires with an expectation of high response it may be that the cost of the postal licence itself and the extra charge for each reply would not be preferable to simply buying stamps and sticking them on the envelopes (tedious though this is). The surveyor must decide according to the particular circumstances; but there is no question at all that payment *must* be made by the sender, not the respondent.

A great problem in sending out postal questionnaires is to decide what to do about following up people who do not reply. A close check should always be kept on the dates when the questionnaires go out. If the surveyor is considering a follow-up to try to boost response then all the questionnaires must have some identifying marks on them, even if they are only serial numbers, otherwise a questionnaire which did not ask for a recipient's name will be unidentifiable. (This is not such an obvious point – I do know of one postal survey in which the sender was so keen to observe anonymity that names and addresses were very explicitly *not* asked for, and with no serial numbers the surveyor then had no idea who had replied and who had not.)

After the questionnaires have been posted there will be a lapse of time before the first replies come trickling in. The trickle will then, one hopes, become a stream, before it gradually declines to a trickle again. It is at the point when the trickle seems to be drying up that a follow-up may be considered. No hard and fast rule as to how many days should elapse after the initial posting date can be given. Some questionnaires may be much longer and more complicated than others, and thus be more likely to take time to complete. It is only likely to annoy recipients if they are reminded of their non-return before they have really had sufficient spare time to deal with them. On the other hand, the longer a person leaves the questionnaire undealt with, the less importance he or she is likely to attach to it, and there comes a point where it really does not seem worth bothering with *now*. The follow-up letter must come before the recipient has reached this 'point of no return', if one may be allowed such an execrable pun.

The actual wording of a follow-up letter must be carefully considered so that recipients are neither abused nor treated as idiots. It needs to be especially courteous and to recognize that the recipient may have been busy, but to stress that a good response rate *is* important and there is still time for the respondent to send back the completed questionnaire. It is a moot point as to whether it is worth sending a second copy of the questionnaire itself at this point. On balance this would seem to suggest that the recipient is a careless person who has managed to lose it in a relatively short period of time, and such an insinuation is rather presumptuous. After the initial sending out and the follow-up it is to be hoped that a good response will have been achieved, and that no more need be done. If the response has been poor in spite of the follow-up, a second follow-up might be considered, but this would be a strong indication of a failed survey. For a recipient to receive three requests from the researcher is going a bit far, and the person who has not responded to the first or second request is not likely to respond to a third.

It would be a pleasant act of courtesy if all the people who return their questionnaires could receive postcards acknowledging receipt of the completed forms and thanking them for their co-operation. Unfortunately this is not likely to be possible since it could well add 50 per cent to the postal costs. Nevertheless, if any public ways of acknowledging assistance given are possible, they should be pursued. Since questionnaire surveys are often used on special groups of people a few lines in, say, a professional journal likely to be read by them is one way of saying thank you. Local surveys are nearly always good for a few lines in the local newspaper and an indication of satisfactory response can be given through this medium. I do not wish to labour the point, but surveyors *are* dependent on the goodwill of their respondents; to leave them feeling satisfied about the help they have given is common courtesy.

DESIGNING QUESTIONNAIRES

Since the problems of question formulation for questionnaires and interview schedules have so much in common we will leave details of the questions themselves for the next chapter. All that needs to be said here is that the general problems of design concerning questionnaires are in some ways much greater than those of designing schedules. The interview schedule is a technical device used by a trained person; if it looks like a cross between a railway timetable and a half-completed game of 'Battleships' this does not matter, so long as the interviewer is helped in asking the right questions and recording the answers properly. By contrast, the questionnaire is likely to be extremely off-putting if it becomes a complicated affair. In any questionnaire space is at a premium and for this reason the printed questionnaire has the advantage of getting more into a given space than a duplicated one and still looking uncrowded; this is apart from the straightforwardly superior attraction of a printed document. A modern typeface, particularly 'sanserif', gives a very clear image and can make a questionnaire aesthetically pleasing. With the spread of computer typesetting and the increasing use of word processors today, it is much easier now for researchers to get well-produced questionnaires at quite reasonable costs. A properly printed questionnaire probably still looks the best of all, but some very good results can be obtained from cheaper methods. Once again, costs will often determine what can be done. If the researcher does become involved in a very large-scale and expensive survey it may well be worthwhile taking advice from a qualified designer who can advise on layout and typeface. The only caution against this is that sometimes they put art before utility, and I personally did not care for one questionnaire I saw where the designer had decided to banish all question marks, on aesthetic grounds. I found the result decidedly difficult to read.

A last point to consider is that questionnaires nearly always have to be folded into envelopes and will receive a fair amount of manhandling before they are dealt with. A good-quality paper is a sensible investment. Not only does the quality surface give a satisfactory appearance, but it means that by the time the document gets to the coders it will not be just a tattered wreck.

SUMMING UP ON QUESTIONNAIRES

The large numbers of surveys which use self-completed questionnaires are adequate testimony to the attractions of this research instrument. However, as I have tried to point out in this chapter, there are problems which should not be ignored in using questionnaires, so let us conclude with a summary of the pros and cons.

Undoubtedly, a great attraction of the self-completed

questionnaire, compared to the interview, is its cheapness. Interviews are expensive in time and labour and therefore are bound to be costly per informant reached. The questionnaire gets the informant to do more of the work for you. When the people to be surveyed are widely spread geographically then the questionnaire may be the obvious method for making contact, since interviews could well be impossibly expensive. In the case of groups of people who gather together in a setting where it is possible to complete questionnaires (such as churches, theatres, libraries, museums and so on), then this technique has some clear advantages.

It can also be argued that one attraction of a well-designed questionnaire is that it is impersonal. By this I mean that there can be no possibility of interviewer bias when there is no interviewer, the respondent does not have to tell a *person* anything and so long as the questionnaire is well designed then respondents do all receive the same stimuli in the same order. This may appear to make the stimulus-response situation rather more 'mechanical', but in some research this may not matter too much. Not every survey needs to probe into people's innermost thoughts and any questionnaire can quite easily include attitude questions and open-ended questions where people write in whatever they want to say.

Against the questionnaire one must accept that its indiscriminate use can result in poor response rates, which may be so poor as to make the survey virtually useless. I well recall a recent survey carried out by university students in which members of staff were asked to complete a questionnaire on their use of certain facilities and no address to which the reply should be sent was given at all! A good response rate is very important in any survey and it is the proportion of replies to numbers of questionnaires that matter, not *just* numbers. One must also be careful not to overload a questionnaire with too many, or too complicated, questions. Every respondent can look through the whole of a questionnaire before even answering the first question and if it seems too much then the response may well be lost all together. Also, in reading through all the questions, the respondent may read into the whole questionnaire certain implications that were never intended. Without an interviewer to keep the responses on the right lines the self-completed questionnaire has a lot of work to do on its own. Of course some people are disinclined to commit themselves to paper anyway and, no matter how much the covering letter may assure them that the replies are anonymous and the forms will be destroyed, recipients may still remain suspicious. Unless the recipients have both an interest and a trust in the purpose of the survey they may well decide not to help. There is too a problem that can arise with questionnaires of people simply entering replies in wrong boxes. Human errors, which an interviewer could easily correct, go uncorrected when the respondent is alone. Thus, a mother of five children, some fully grown, might mistakenly tick her own age as 'under 21', which would be patently absurd. The questionnaire itself cannot query this error.

Generally speaking, the self-completed questionnaire is a very valuable research tool which should be used carefully and with discrimination. It is best suited for particular groups of people who are spaced geographically and who may be expected to have an interest in the topic under survey. It cannot get the 'depth' that a good personal interview can achieve, but it is very well suited to 'breadth' and can include interesting, and even stimulating, questions if it is well designed.

We will now look in detail at how to ask questions.

8

How to Ask Questions

In the two previous chapters we have discussed some of the problems that arise in trying to ask the right question in the right way, and in chapter 6 we touched on some of the specific dangers which must be guarded against if questions are to be satisfactorily asked, answered and analysed. In this chapter we shall take a more detailed look at some of the problems that are common to both interview schedules and self-completed questionnaires. First of all we shall have a look at some of the particular problems that have to be coped with in the detailed framing of questions and then, using a specially devised 'spoof' interview schedule which contains a large number of faults, we can try our own skills in a game of 'spot the deliberate mistake'.

SOME GENERAL POINTS

Bowley's warning (noted in chapter 6) against asking too many questions is a good starting point for any questionnaire or schedule designer. There is little point in asking respondents for information which is readily available from other sources. One is likely to want to know the sex of a respondent in most enquiries, but it would be disastrous to the success of an interview for the *interviewer* to ask this question of an informant. Where observation is sufficient it is silly to verbalize a question. Quite often in interviews it is possible to obtain information about respondents' marital status, occupation, place of residence, and so on, during general questioning, which is one good reason for leaving classificatory data until the end of the interview when not only does it seem less instrusive, but also some details may have already been given. Unfortunately this cannot be done when self-completed questionnaires are used and so the general problem of how much or how little to ask for must be carefully considered.

All questions that qualify for inclusion in a survey must earn their keep − they must produce something of value to justify their being asked in the first place. So the criterion of relevance is fundamental to the inclusion of any question. The questionnaire designer must know what use is to be made of the replies when they are ready for analysis. It is easy enough to throw questions and answers away when you realize that you do not know how to analyse them, but this is a very wasteful procedure and hardly fair to one's respondents who have given time and energy to supplying answers.

Another problem with question-asking is that questions can so easily get too complicated. When people are asked about their past history, with very detailed probling into their periods in particular jobs or times they lived in particular areas, there is a danger of asking respondents to try to work back to times they had practically forgotten about − and it may well be that the detail asked for is really not at all necessary for analysis. Very often the analysis itself is going to be in categories anyway, so if thought has been given to the analysis categories *before* the survey goes out into the field then the analysis categories become the response categories straightaway. Thus, for example, if one asks a person how many years they have been a member of an organization it could be quite difficult for them to work out *exactly* how many years they have been a member. But if the analysis is going to be in categories such as (a) under a year, (b) 1 to 4 years, (c) 5 to 9 years, (d) 10 to 14 years, (e) 15 to 19 years, (f) 20 years or more, then the respondent has an easier, and quicker, task of choosing the appropriate 'box' for response. In a similar way respondents can be helped in expressing opinions by the interviewer putting the question to them and asking them to say, of an interest, whether they hold this interest 'very strongly', 'fairly strongly', 'only slightly' or 'not at all'. The words themselves can vary according to circumstances; the point is to make it clear to respondents that they are only being asked to express a categorical form of response — not to give an oration on the topic. Wording of questions, however, is very important indeed and it is essential that the survey designer works for clarity and conciseness in question phrasing.

My favourite example of the question that got completely out of hand was one thought up by a student on a projected survey of the social and religious aspects of the rite of baptism. It went, 'Would you agree that in some measure the official ceremony of baptism plays a part in establishing the dual role played by husband and wife in responsibility for the child, after the emphasis on the feminine aspect at the actual birth?' If you read this question slowly it is perfectly sensible, but to ask it like this in an interview would make it sound like a philosophical treatise and to print it on a self-completed questionnaire would make it look like a mini-thesis. In the same project another question suggested was 'If the child had godparents, what was the prior relation between godparents and the children or the parents?' This question is not too bad until we get to the last three words when tacking on the 'or the parents' bit throws the whole question into confusion. Generally speaking, therefore, questions in interviews or questionnaires which result in the respondent having to stop to try to make a tricky calculation or to work out what a question actually means should be re-phrased at a preparatory stage. It is quite useful at times, just before piloting, to ask a colleague or friend to pretend to be a member of the sample to be surveyed and to respond to or complete the questions you have drafted. The results can often be most useful. All interviews and questionnaires should have a good 'flow' about them and anything that can be done to facilitate this is worth the effort.

It is also dangerous to overestimate the intelligence of one's respondents when asking questions. it is a very corny joke that expresses dismay at the fact that half the population is below average intelligence — and one has to know which average is being used to accept the statement anyway. But it must be remembered that in any *general* survey of the population the majority of the respondents will not be well educated or accustomed to dealing with abstract concepts. It can therefore be thoughtless, and embarrassing to respondents, if questions are asked which are beyond the grasp of the people in the sample. This danger can only be overcome by careful scrutiny of questions, and although it does not mean that the question designer should treat all respondents as near imbeciles it does mean that the designer has to be aware that his own expertise and interest in the field of enquiry is not going to be found in the respondents. Once again it must be stressed that the exploratory and pilot stages of surveys should deal with these problems so that when the final version of the schedule or questionnaire is drafted these pitfalls will already have been dealt with.

Having made these general points, which are common to both schedules and questionnaires, let us now look at points of detail, some of which have been introduced in chapter 6.

SOME POINTS OF DETAIL

'When did you stop beating your wife?' is probably the best-known example of a badly phrased question since it is based on an assumption which is probably not tenable in 99.9 per cent of cases. But while wife-beating is an obviously tricky area for question asking, other simpler areas still have their dangers. Without going into detail too much let us consider five problems of question asking and then try our hands at the 'spoof' interview schedule.

(1) *Ambiguous questions*. These are questions in which the phrasing results in the respondent being able to make more than one interpretation of the question. Few students need instruction in spotting the *double entrendre* in a lecture — as every lecturer knows to his cost. It is a basic necessity in question framing that the question put shall have one meaning, and one meaning only, to all the respondents, no matter how many they may be. A good example of ambiguity can be seen in a question on people's reading habits which asked 'How long is it since you borrowed a book?' The respondent was given seven set response categories to tick which could cover all eventualities from 'within the past week' to 'never borrow at all'. However, although it was virtually certain that the questionnaire designer had meant the question to refer *only* to borrowing from a library, and probably in this survey a public library, the question did not say this. It is known from other researches that many people borrow novels, especially light paperback fiction, from friends and relations and it would be perfectly reasonable for a respondent to regard this as borrowing when answering this question. In the survey of visitors to the British Museum we wanted to know what sort of transport people had used to get to the museum. The problem is that some people staying in nearby hotels could have walked and so we needed a category of 'walked'. But then virtually everyone could say that they walked to the museum, even if it was only from the nearest bus-stop or tube station, so it was necessary to give interviewers special instructions to ensure that everyone interviewed understood what was meant by the term 'walked'. There is, of course, the silly story of the questionnaire that asked married couples 'When your first child was born did you want a boy or a girl?' and one hundred per cent of respondents answered 'yes'!

(2) *Leading questions*. These are questions which, in the very way they are put, tend to influence the answer that a person gives. They are particularly important in attitude or opinion questions where a particular point at issue should

always be presented from a central, or neutral starting point. To begin a question 'Do you agree that . . .' is to require a positive disagreement on the part of the respondent, and this is not an impartial way of presenting questions. Where there is an answer that can indicate yes/no or agree/disagree it is only fair to give the respondent an evenly balanced choice. Perhaps the simplest way to try to achieve neutrality is to put the question as 'Do you agree or disagree with the statement that . . .' Then, for response categories, the respondent can be given a choice of 'strongly agree', 'moderately agree', 'neutral', 'moderately disagree' and 'strongly disagree'. It is, in these cases, also useful to allow for the person who does not feel he can offer an opinion and so a category for the 'don't knows' is helpful.

(3) *Double questions.* One might think that it is very easy to avoid double questions, since they must be obvious, but this is not always so. In trying to reduce the number of questions on a schedule or questionnaire, or in trying to save a small amount of space, the designer often thinks that an economy can be made by putting two questions together. The result is likely to be a double question which cannot be answered by one response. A simple example would be asking a person 'How often do you go to the cinema or theatre?' The answer is obviously: so often to the cinema, and so often to the theatre, but a *simple* answer to this one question could well be impossible and certainly if attempted would be virtually meaningless. Another common example might be to ask a person in a reading survey if his or her parents were book readers. This question would itself require a careful phrasing but it is obvious that anyone could have parents of whom one was a reader and the other was not. A double question with only one possible response does not work.

(4) *Jargon and technical terms.* Sociologists are often criticized, and often rightly so, for using jargon when plain English would make communication much easier. Perhaps this does not matter so much between sociologists who understand the language of sociologese, but for commuication

between sociologists and respondents the onus is always on the researcher to find words which can be understood by the respondent; if he fails to do this such thoughtlessness deserves a lack of response. It may be all right to talk to sociologists about 'kinship networks', but it is probably better to ask a bank clerk about her 'relatives'. To ask a married person the question, which I once saw in a draft questionnaire, 'Do you cohabit with your spouse?' would surely baffle many ordinary people who had unknowingly been doing just that for years. A questionnaire about work which asks a person if he or she 'holds an executive position' is likely to raise difficulties, since 'executive position' can be so very differently interpreted. Perhaps this second example is as much one of ambiguity as technicality, but whatever label one attaches to it, it is not a good question. When dealing with surveys which involve organizations one must take great care not to assume that members understand all the complex workings of the organization. It is pointless asking lay people their opinions of the working of 'advisory' or 'consultative' committees if these bodies are unknown to them. Good pilot work can eliminate such confusing and unhelpful questions.

(5) *Emotional questions.* We have already noted that interviews and self-completed questionnaires depend on honest replies. One source of replies which may well not be honest is the question which gets the respondent emotionally involved. Question askers must take especial care in such delicate areas as sexual behaviour, religion, politics and social class. Where there are 'oughts' of behaviour in society, or a certain group within society, respondents may well tend to give the answer which they think they 'ought' to give, rather than the answer which tells what they actually do. Thus, questions on smoking, drinking, gambling and drug-taking (always depending on the circumstances under which questions are put) are always likely to result in replies which under-state the reality. The person who is asked how many cigarettes he smokes a day is likely to give a figure on the low side rather than the high side, since cigarette smoking is

dangerous to health, wasteful of money and often a nuisance to other people. It would be rather an act of defiance to over-state one's daily cigarette consumption. On the other hand, if people are asked how many books they read a week, a month, or a year, they are likely to over-state since book reading in most circles carries prestige rather than oppro-brium.[1] Now cigarette smoking and book reading are not highly charged emotional areas, but they are nevertheless commonplace aspects of life about which 'oughts' may well have importance. A study of social mobility which asked a young graduate 'Do you think your father is of lower social class than yourself?' might well be very much to the heart of the matter under investigation, but it would be an extremely hard question to take without embarrassment. To ask a businessman 'How often do you visit prostitutes when you are on business in London?' might throw an interesting light on managerial behaviour, but a very special type of interview would be needed for this sort of question. Emotions vary enormously among different people in different situ-ations. There was a time when it was regarded as rather poor taste to ask people if they were divorced and so the categories used were sometimes 'single', 'married', 'widowed' and a euphemistic 'other'. Now there seems to be no problem at all about asking people if they are divorced and I have recently seen a questionnaire using the category 'partner' for unmarried couples living together. There is also a problem which some-times arises in trying to ascribe social status by the use of occupational categories. For married people who both work it is sometimes the case that the husband has a higher-status occupation than his wife. If the wife's status is ranked then she would appear to be of lower social status than her husband. This problem is quite a serious technical matter which stems from trying to assess status by occupation in the first place, but for our purposes at the moment it should be noted that while at one time it was possible to ask a married woman to give her husband's occupation in questionnaires or interviews, it is now quite likely to be regarded as insulting by more liberated and independent wives. I have come across an interviewer who objected to the very use of the category 'housewife', as she regarded the term as degrading. Happily, not all housewives feel so. It is clear, though, that it is hard to generalize about emotional questions. Perhaps the best advice one can give is to reiterate the earlier warning to the question asker to try hard to think of the likely reaction from the respondent. Not to do this can lead to difficult situations.

A PRACTICAL ILLUSTRATION

Some years ago my students were engaged with me on a survey into certain social aspects of local shopping. As part of the exercise all the students tried their hand at devising an interview schedule which was to be used for home interviews with people who did the main grocery shopping for the household. The various attempts contained, as first attempts always do, a good number of badly constructed questions. From these I put together, with very little embellishment of my own, the following interview schedule. It is full of errors of all sorts, and when I have gone through it with succeeding intakes of students we always seem to be able to find a few further faults which had not been noted before. I think one can almost go on for ever, depending on how pernickety you want to be. No schedule or questionnaire is ever perfect and on points of fine detail there will always be room for personal disagreements as to how things could be improved. I suggest to the reader that you do not spend too much time on this 'spoof' schedule; it is mainly given here so that you can exercise your wits in spotting the grosser errors. When you have picked them out you will find a list given of the major ones. If you have found genuine errors of a gross type not mentioned in this list, give yourself a few bonus marks but don't go away feeling too smug — it is easy to tear other people's work to shreds, but probably not so easy to produce a first-class alternative. If you don't think so, then I suggest you try your hand at re-phrasing all the bad questions you have criticized. The job of reconstruction will be a longer one than the job of demolition. It is a sad fact of life that it takes very little time to pull a building down, but it takes a great deal of thought, care and time to put one up. Demolition experts do not always make the best survey designers.

Shopping Survey

To Interviewers

Call at houses on your list and obtain interview with woman who does the principal shopping. Explain that you are from University Department of Sociology and that you are carrying out a survey into people's attitudes to counter-service and self-service grocers.

1 What is your age?   −20 ☐   20–30 ☐   30–40 ☐
    40–50 ☐   50–60 ☐   60–70 ☐   70 and over ☐

2 What is your marital status?
        Married ☐   Single ☐   Widowed ☐

3 Have you any dependent children?   Yes/No
    If yes, how many?   1   2   3   4   5   6   7   or more

4 How long have you lived in this district?   . . . years

5 Where do you buy your main groceries?
    . . . .

6 Is it counter-service or self-service?
            S/S ☐   C/S ☐

7 Have you always shopped there?   Yes/No

8 Do you know, or are you known by, the shop assistants?
    Yes/No

9 Do you consider shopping to be a tedious necessity or do you gain enjoyment from it?   Yes/No/Don't know

10 When you go shopping, which of the following attitudes is foremost in your mind?
    (a) It's got to be done   . . . .
    (b) I might meet Mrs So-and-so and have a chat . . . .
    (c) It will be a pleasant break from housework . . . .
    (d) I might look for good value   . . . .

11 When buying groceries, do you prefer to
    (a) buy a few items at a time?   . . . .
    (b) buy the whole week's groceries at one time? . . . .

12 At the grocer's which you patronize, do you also buy meat, fruit and vegetables? Yes/No

With particular regard to counter-service and self-service grocers:

13 Do you feel that *you* could steal from a self-service grocers if you so wished? Yes/No
Do you think it would be easy to steal? Yes/No
If NO, why not? . . . .
. . . .

14 Which type of shop do you feel freer and more independent in?
C/S ☐ S/S ☐

15 Do you associate either type of shop with a class concept?
Yes ☐ No ☐

16 Do you feel that you are tempted to buy more in a self-service shop because the goods look more tempting or do you feel that because there is a wide range of choice you can buy the exact amount you can afford?
. . . .

17 Do you feel goods are likely to be fresher in a self-service shop, due possibly to higher turnover? Yes/No

18 Do you think branded goods are cheaper in a self-service shop, and thus you get more value for money? Yes/No

19 Do you consider that the self-service shop stocks a wider variety of goods than the ordinary grocer? Yes/No

20 Do you regard the counter-service grocery shop as a traditional form which has given good service for a long time? Yes/No

21 Do you think of the self-service shop as something large and impersonal and not really requiring the loyalty that would be afforded to a small grocer who you know? Yes/No

22 Do you agree with the following statements?
(a) Self-service shops are cheap, efficient and clean.
Yes/No
(b) Self-service shops are expensive, inefficient and unhygenic.
Yes/No
(c) Counter-service shops are friendly, warm and personal.
Yes/No
(d) Assistants in counter-service shops are always more helpful and efficient than in self-service shops.
Yes/No

(e) You can pop into a counter-service shop for occasional items, but you have to buy in larger quantities in a self-service shop. Yes/No

23 Do you go out to work? Yes/No

24 Do you have a car? Yes/No

25 What social class would you say you were?
Working ☐ Lower-middle ☐ Middle ☐ Upper-middle ☐

Comments on the shopping schedule

A general point to begin: the first three questions cover what we call classificatory data, necessary for analysis of respondents' social characteristics but not obviously relevant to them so far as the object of the survey is concerned. These questions are best left till last when they can be used as 'finishing-off questions' when respondents have got used to answering questions. With a woman in particular it is poor tactics to ask her age in the very first question. Actually people nowadays very rarely raise any difficulties over this question, but it is certainly best left until a little 'rapport' has been established.

1 The wording 'What is your age?' is very formal. An interviewer would more naturally ask 'Do you mind if I ask how old you are?' This could be put down on the schedule as simply 'How old are you?' and the interviewer can add a suitable preparatory phrase. The response categories are faulty since they overlap. A person aged exactly 30, 40, 50 or 60 could be ticked in two boxes. To make these age ranges suitable for analysis purposes they should be 20–29, 30–39, and so on.

2 A person actually asked 'What is your marital status?' might well be baffled as to what this meant, and could even be very insulted. 'Marital status' is a technical term. Far better to ask 'Are you single, married, widowed or divorced?' Quite often it is fairly apparent in an

interview that a person is not single, so this can be left out if it is obviously not appropriate. People living together may be treated as married for the survey purposes if they live as married people. In certain surveys, however, these people might be treated as specially interesting cases and categorized separately. The important thing is to define the category clearly and stick to it throughout. Note also that the order of the boxes would be more logical if the order went from 'Single' to 'Married', which is a natural progression, rather than hopping back from 'Married' to 'Single'. 'Divorced' can be the fourth category.

3 'Dependent children' may well baffle many people, so the question needs to be phrased so that children are sorted out into the categories needed for analysis purposes. For the survey probably categories of 'pre-school', 'at school, living at home' and any other categories such as 'education, away from home' or 'working, living at home' would be meaningful. These, then, would need to be categorized for the response so that a table on the schedule would seem to be useful. It would also be better to instruct the interviewers that this question should be asked only of married or widowed women. There may be single women with dependent children, but it is best for this to come out later in the interview, as it surely will. The direct confrontation of unmarried women with this question would lose goodwill. Note also that there are no instructions to interviewers about how to complete the answers to this question. Questions 1 and 2 had boxes to be ticked but this one does not. It would be better to have boxes again for the 'yes' and the 'no'; the actual numbers of children could be ringed so long as there *is* an instruction so to do. It is also useful. when a question has a subsidiary question for some respondents, to help the interviewer by drawing attention to this. In question 3 it would help if the 'If yes' were to be printed in bold

type (if possible) and certainly to have it in capitals as 'IF YES'.

4 A question of this type can be a useful starter to an interview so long as it does not necessitate complicated calculations. If the analysis categories have been pre-determined the interviewer can help by suggesting such categories as 'under 5 years', '5 but less than 10', and so on, to save the respondent doing useless calculatons. Probably the easiest way to put this question would be to say 'Have you lived in this district very long? – under 5 years? 5 but less than 10?' This makes it much easier for the respondent to give a general answer. The problem with the actual question as it is phrased here is that 'this district' is too vague. People move around within towns and cities and subjective ideas of districts vary. Probably 'this house' would be better, though if the research were being done in a very clearly defined district, it might be possible to say 'in Lower Fulbrook', or whatever the name was.

5 This question rather presupposes that people (a) stick to one shop, (b) do have a 'main' grocer. A re-phrasing to take into account these points would probably use some specific regular purchases (such as fats) and would ask where these were normally bought. But buying patterns (especially when groceries are delivered, or where people call at supermarkets on their way home) can vary enormously and probably more than one question would have to be asked in order to establish various types of shoppers for analysis purposes. These types could probably be ascertained in a pilot survey and could then be used as set answers for the interviewer to check. Probably a class of 'Other, specify . . .' would be needed for people with very individual habits. The main point here is *not* to collect everybody's individual little differences, but to try to work out a limited number of useful categories of shoppers – useful, that is, for analysis purposes. This question, therefore,

really needs complete re-thinking, since a respondent who *does* have the one grocer from whom she buys all her groceries will reply by saying what the name and address of the shop is, and these facts are not really going to be analysed.

6 If the problem of question 5 can be solved, then this question seeks to find out whether the 'regular' grocer is a self-service or counter-service type. For reliable answers to this the respondent needs to be given a little explanation so that there is no doubt whatsoever as to what the two terms mean. Note also that the response boxes here are in reverse order to the way in which the question is put. If counter-service precedes self-service in the question it is better to have that order for the response, otherwise it is virtually certain that in the heat of the interview some interviewer will tick in the self-service box because it comes first when they really mean to tick in the counter-service one. Note also that 'S/S' and 'C/S' are abbreviations which are not necessary. There is plenty of room on this line for the full wording.

7 The word 'always' is absolutely meaningless. The interviewer wants some idea of how long the informant has shopped there, so a question must be framed on these lines, with appropriate response categories in mind. A problem that could pose difficulties here is that the shop itself may be a new one, or it might, in recent years, have changed over from counter- to self-service. Note too that, once again, there are no boxes for ticking 'yes' or 'no' and this is a continuing fault throughout the questionnaire which need not be mentioned again. Responses *can* be ringed but boxes with ticks in them are rather more definite and remind the interviewer more strongly.

8 The word 'know' can be interpreted in a multitude of ways, especially in its biblical sense. In this context it is ambiguous to the point of being meaningless. I may

'know' that a shop assistant lives at a certain house in a road, but this means little in the context of shopping. Also, this is a double question. The respondent may well believe she 'knows' the assistants, but they may not 'know' her. More specific, objective terms are needed.

9 The wording for the two alternatives is rather extreme, especially 'tedious necessity', and it does not give a happy choice anyway. Shopping is obviously a 'necessity' but people still gain enjoyment from necessities. The major error, however, lies in the response categories, since a yes or a no is absolutely meaningless as a reply to the question put.

10 This is an example of a question which is put to the respondent with a selection of answers actually suggested. The respondent can be given two alternatives; either she indicates *all* the answers with which she agrees, or else must choose only one which is paramount. This question asks for one answer (*foremost* in the respondent's mind) but gives a choice which is not conducive to picking out one. A housewife could answer yes to all four of the suggestions but she would have great difficulty in deciding if any one suggestion could be said to be 'foremost in her mind' since the four ideas are of different kinds, not a series of gradations of one idea. Also, this question is an example of the need to 'prompt' the respondent by offering set choices to select from. In some cases this can be done verbally, but with four topics such as these a 'prompt' card, which could be handed to the respondent to look at, would certainly help. In fact this question would be better if the four responses were *not* considered against each other but were dealt with one by one and the respondent could be asked how strongly she felt about (a), (b), (c) and (d), one by one, using simple category responses such as 'very much', 'fairly much', 'not much' and 'not at all'. (Incidentally, I have been told that

'fairly much' is totally ungrammatical. However, I consider it is easily understood and therefore useful and I am unrepentant.)

11 This is mainly at fault for giving only two extreme choices and leaving out an obvious middle one of the person who buys more than just a few items more than once a week. However, this is also a good example of a question that is very difficult to ask at all since people's shopping preferences can vary so much with their living patterns. To get a really useful analysis one would probably have to split this question up more.

12 An example of a triple question. Only a yes or a no is recorded whereas three yes/no categories are needed for the meat, the fruit and the vegetables. Also, just try saying this question out loud and see how pompous it sounds. In this context the word 'patronize' sounds archaic.

Between question 12 and question 13: this is actually a break point in the interview at which the interviewer is going to tell the respondent that the next few questions are about counter-service and self-service grocers' shops in particular. It would be better, therefore, if there was a distinct gap between this opening remark and the preceding question 12 and to have this intro-duction in bold type or capitals would remind the interviewer of what is coming next.

13 This question was genuinely suggested, based on the fact that pilfering is common in many self-service shops. It would, however, be very unfortunate to place such a blunt question as this before most honest shop-pers and both embarrassment and anger could be the result.

14 This question demonstrates an instance where the question asker obviously has an idea that could be interesting but has not thought about the problems it could pose for the person trying to answer it. To feel 'free' and 'independent' in a grocer's shop would seem

very odd to some people. Certainly, to less intelligent respondents, this question could seem very odd.

15 A beautiful example of sociological jargon. The very wording is reminiscent of some of the worst sociological writing. It also presumes that ordinary people think of everything in terms of social class, which is a dubious presumption anyway.

16 I suggested to my students that this question could well have a pre-coded response category of 'Eh?' One sees what the questioner had in mind, but put in these actual words the result could be hilarious. Like the previous example of the question on baptism, this one shows a lack of thought for the respondents. The question compiler may know what it means, but it is unlikely that an ordinary shopper will be able to disentangle it.

17 This would be all right as one question about fresher goods in self-service shops, but the addition of one possible reason complicates the whole issue and makes a response impossible in simple yes/no terms. Also, this is a leading question which suggests to the respondent that goods are fresher in self-service shops. To avoid leading the respondent it should also be suggested that goods could be less fresh, or no different at all.

18 This is the same problem as in question 17, of asking a question and then requiring a particular reason to be accepted with it.

19 This, like questions 17 and 18, is a leading question which expects the answer 'yes', unless the respondent is prepared to make a special effort at denying the positive suggestion put. Questions 17 and 18 were rather obscured by being difficult in other ways, but all three questions are very clearly biased towards the self-service shop.

20 This question is biased the other way — towards the counter-service shop — and manages to be double as well. It also contains a description of the counter-

service as being 'a traditional form' which is not a very clear concept anyway.

21 This is another example of a long, involved question which is leading and double at the same time. The phrasing of 'loyalty that would be afforded' is somewhat pompous and it equates counter-service with 'small', which is questionable and obviously intended to arouse sympathy for the underdog. Also, the word 'requiring' is wrong; probably the compiler meant something more like 'arousing' or 'creating'.

22 This clearly should lead off with a choice between agreeing or disagreeing with statements which follow; as it stands the respondent is almost challenged to disagree, if he or she has the courage. The questions (a), (b) and (c) are triple ones since, for example, a shop can be clean but not cheap or efficient, and so on. Question (d) is double; probably many of us know helpful assistants who are not efficient. Also, the extreme word 'always' would probably be too dogmatic for most people. Question (e) is difficult to understand because the two concepts offered are not mutually exclusive and the words 'occasional items' are most obscure. The idea is there but re-phrasing is needed.

23 Before moving from the questions about shopping to questions of a personal nature, a line of instructions to interviewers would be wise, with a suggested linking phrase such as 'I am now going to leave shopping and I want to ask a few questions about you yourself.' Question 23 itself is very simple in wording, but a 'yes' reply could mean so many different things that it is unlikely to be adequate. The point of importance in this survey is that a housewife who does go out to work at all could have patterns of shopping which might be strongly affected by the hours she works, the place where she works, how she gets to work, and so on. A simple yes/no to this question is likely to be

grossly inadequate for analysis purposes and suggests that the survey designer has not thought much about what he intends to do with this answer when he comes to the analysis stage. Certainly, as it stands, the interviewers will have to write in all sorts of responses which will be difficult to code after the survey.

24 This is another rather bald question which suggests a number of further necessary questions. The word 'you' could be interpreted as meaning either the respondent alone, or the respondent and spouse, with resulting gross errors in responses. Many middle-class housewives have their own personal car; many more have regular use of the family car for shopping. The question is clearly asked because the researcher wants to know about the use of a car for shopping, but this question does not ask about that at all.

25 This question, as set out here, is a rather frontal attack on a somewhat emotional topic. If an *objective* measure of social status is to be used for analysis the husband's occupation is normally used. If *subjective* social class is to be used, by a respondent's self-rating, then some objective criteria are normally required for check purposes. As this question stands it is in a somewhat crude form and there is no indication to interviewers as to whether the four categories are to be suggested to informants or whether, if the informant gives an unprompted answer, the interviewer should tick the nearest box which he or she considers most appropriate. Where a prompt is to be given it is usual for the interview schedule to have the word 'PROMPT' clearly displayed.

GENERAL REMARKS

It is not possible in an introductory textbook of this length to deal with every type of problem which arises when framing questions for interview schedules or questionnaires. You can best develop expertise by examining critically as many schedules and questionnaires as you can find and by gathering together your own personal collection. These should include not only academic ones used in university research projects but also commercial ones, many of which are extremely interesting and well-designed. Manufacturers quite often ask customers to complete questionnaires on goods they have purchased and I have in my own collection well-designed questionnaires from a motor car manufacturer and a refrigerator firm. Travel firms also ask customers to complete questionnaires for them and these too can be very interesting. I have also a small collection of questionnaires left in hotel rooms for guests to complete, asking for their views on the facilities and services supplied. I feel these are likely to attract a disproportionate response from the dissatisfied customers, yet this may be helpful to the proprietors.[2] Magazines and newspapers too sometimes ask their readers to complete questionnaires for them and at times these are less than expertly designed, but all are grist to the mill of the student who wants to learn how to ask questions.

It is very desirable, when surveys are written up in book or report form, that they should include with the results a copy of the questionnaire or schedule used, in an appendix. If this is not done it is by no means a bad idea to write to the author asking for a copy for oneself. (When doing this it should be remembered that a self-addressed envelope with stamp may well produce a better response.) Unfortunately, it is rarely feasible for journals to reproduce questionnaires or schedules, but authors of research papers are nearly always pleased to have people take an interest in their work and a request for a questionnaire is unlikely to be refused. But, once again, while a critical approach to other people's work is desirable, it is equally important to be able to work constructively oneself. So, whenever one finds a poor question, the real benefit will come not merely from spotting the error but from going on from there and producing an improved version of it.

At the risk of being tedious, I would reiterate two points which have already been strongly made in previous pages but which I feel cannot be over-stressed. The first is that the survey designer, when asking questions, must constantly think of the *respondent* rather than himself. It is the respondent who will give the answers to an interviewer or who will complete the questionnaire for you. Everything depends on the goodwill, the honesty and the co-operation of the respondent. No respondents means no results. Confused respondents means bad results. So point 1, never to be set aside, is that the respondent must never be forgotten.

Not very long ago I received a questionnaire from someone carrying out a survey on a subject in which I am involved. At one stage the questionnaire said 'If you have answered (3c) with 'helpful' please proceed with question 4'. In fact the reference was to (5c), not (3c); the words used were 'useful' or 'unnecessary', not 'helpful' or 'unhelpful' and the next question was 6, and 4. The person who had designed the questionnaire had obviously altered it at some pilot stage but had not checked it through for the consequent alterations necessary in both question numbers and words used. This placed the onus on the respondent to work out what was wrong with the instructions, and it is not the job of respondents to correct questionnaires as well as to complete them.

Point 2 is that surveys are used to ask questions which will produce replies and those replies have to be analysed. Until one has been through several surveys it is difficult to appreciate the amount of work that *should* go into preparation for analysis. The tyro surveyor who takes an attitude of 'Let's get on with the survey and we'll bother about the analysis later' is heading for real trouble. Preparation done for the analysis stage *before* the survey itself is carried out is crucial and in the next chapter I hope to show why this is so.

9

Analysis and Presentation
of Results

INTRODUCTION

In previous pages dealing with the various ways in which questions can be asked it has been stressed throughout that questions are themselves only stimuli and it is the responses that matter. Every survey enquiry ends up with a number of completed interview schedules or questionnaires. The number may be under a hundred, in the case of an undergraduate dissertation (or even a more advanced study of respondents in depth), or it may result in several thousand replies. In my own six-week survey of a theatre audience the complete response was near to 12,000 questionnaires and storage alone was a problem, even before analysis began.

It is, therefore, vitally important to consider as early as possible in a survey how material is going to be analysed and presented. If the study stems, as it should do in sociological enquiry, from the wish to test a hypothesis, or to refine a theory or a concept, then there is a pattern which is determined by the problem itself. Not every sociological enquiry entails a social survey. Many sociological enquiries use documentary sources, often of a historical type. These studies may eventually lead to empirical field enquiries, but in many cases they do not and they are none the worse for it. Indeed, it is highly desirable for researchers to recognize that a field survey is only to be undertaken if the nature of the enquiry necessitates information being gained through this method. Surveys are hard work, time-consuming and often expensive; there is no sense in dashing into them without thought for what they will achieve and why they are necessary for the research which is being carried out. Research requires data to test hypotheses which may advance theories, but the data needed may well be obtainable from published sources if one knows how to go about locating those sources. A great deal of research can be successfully completed working at the desk, using what can be called 'library' resources. It is therefore imperative that the research worker knows about sources of information in his chosen subject area and also knows how to locate and obtain them. The researcher who has no knowledge of how to use indexing and abstracting journals could well get involved in wasteful empirical survey ventures.

If this warning is kept in mind then many surveys can be avoided altogether and alternative, perhaps better, sources of data can be used. Where surveys do appear to be necessary they will show themselves to be necessary because of the *answers* they will provide to important questions. The researcher must be clear in his mind about what he wants to find out. Social research is often about people's characteristics and natures. *Who* are the people who involve themselves in this sort of activity and *what* are the reasons for them doing so? The answers needed to these big questions will be given by a series of smaller questions providing a series of answers which, sensibly put together, give the social researcher as good an answer altogether as can be got with the resources available. Good social research, like good commercial business, aims for a high return on investment, and poorly planned research, like poorly planned business ventures, is often wasteful of limited resources. This is not to suggest that a survey designer should expect that every question asked is going to produce evidence of world-shattering importance. Much social research does confirm expected hypotheses: an experienced market researcher once expressed to me that he usually knew in advance the broad answers to the questions he was researching, but what was important for his clients was the degree of accuracy he would attain in measuring those answers. A lot of social research is like this market research – we already have some general ideas about *what* people do and, perhaps, *why* they do, before we conduct a survey, but we feel we need to go further than our current resources and to seek out the answers to new questions.

All this adds up to the important point, which has already been made but which there is no harm in repeating, that if a question is asked with no idea at all in advance of what the likely answer will be, then it is highly likely that the researcher has not given enough thought to what he is asking that question *for*. Questions are only included in a survey when the question designer has already some fair idea of what answers are likey to come back and what general outline of analysis will be imposed on them.

PRE-CODING OF QUESTIONS

Social research is inherently quantitative, even though some people do not like to acknowledge that analysing social behaviour is really a numbers game. One can hardly make any sensible social statement without implicitly or explicitly involving ideas which are, at base, quantitative. When sociologists refer to 'the middle classes' of a society they have categorized certain people in that society according to certain criteria which mark them off from other people, such as 'the working classes'. If these classes are to have any useful meaning at all then we must know of what class proportions the society referred to is made up. If, say, 95 per cent of a society were middle class this would be a very different society from one in which only 5 per cent of the people were middle class. When public library statistics refer to 'registered borrowers' they may mean people who have actually borrowed books within the past year in some library authority areas, but in others they could include people who have had bor-rowers' tickets for years and never been inside the library. Classification depends upon definition and clear and useful classification can be achieved by forethought when surveying. If surveyors ask themselves how they will use the answers to their questions then they are well on the way to employ-ing sensible classifications.

For example, questions on what members of a family do in their leisure time will obviously need to discriminate between members of the families surveyed and so sex, marital status and age will almost certainly be necessary variables for analysing other activities. Let us begin with the variable of sex. There is no problem here of deciding what response categories to use since all respondents will be male or female. In a schedule or questionnaire boxes labelled 'Male' and 'Female' can be included without fear of them being inadequate and the surveyor can go on to think of the ways in which analysis of other factors according to sex may be used to test hypotheses or set down necessary basic information. Marital status will normally be dealt with by boxes labelled 'Single', 'Married', 'Widowed' and 'Divorced', and these categories should be sufficiently definitive unless it is deemed necessary to include a special category for 'Separated', if the survey is looking particularly at problems of family breakdown. The purpose of the enquiry will always dictate the particular analysis categories to be used. When we come to age we have a continuous rather than a discrete variable and the analysis categories to be used could be of any size at all. The decision as to whether to use, say, a five-year or a ten-year age category can only be decided on the basis of what ideas are being tested. If there is any doubt it is probably best to leave set categories aside and simply use an open box or line on which the interviewer or respondent can enter the actual age in years. Classification of this answer can be done afterwards at the analysis stage. The important point is that by giving a respondent a set of answers to check on a questionnaire, or by giving a set of responses for an interviewer to tick, ring or underline on a schedule, one can save writing in of answers and thus avoid the ambiguities (or even illegible handwriting) which make subsequent analysis difficult. The situation is more important in a self-completed questionnaire than an interview since interviewers can be instructed as to what answers to expect and how to enter them on the schedule, but the person filling in a questionnaire cannot be made to read a whole sheet of instructions and so as many 'hidden' instructions as possible should be incorporated in the questions themselves by means of set response categories.

For example, in one of my first surveys of theatre audiences, carried out at the Sheffield Playhouse theatre, I wanted to try to find out how the people in the audience had first found out that the play they were watching was going to be produced at this theatre. Exploratory research, which included questioning the publicity officer and carrying out a pilot survey, had indicated the most likely sources and these were printed on the questionnaire so as to help respondents choose, as far as possible, their own particular sources. To have asked respondents to write in their own answers would probably have resulted in far too many un-analysable responses such as 'an advertisement' or 'I heard about it'. The set answer, we hoped, would overcome these ambiguous or vague replies.

How did you first learn that this play was being produced at the Playhouse?

(1) Newspaper advertisement ☐   (5) Indoor notice/poster   ☐
(2) Outdoor poster ☐   (6) From a friend   ☐
(3) Playhouse mailing list ☐   (7) From a relative   ☐
(4) Programme notes ☐   (8) Don't know   ☐

(9) Other means, please say how . . . .

The above set of answers meant that in analysing the replies nine pre-determined categories would be used and it can be seen that statistical tables could easily be constructed to test hypotheses about where people first learned of this play. For instance, suppose we hypothesized that older people heard about the play more from personal recommendation, while younger people learned about it more through formal advertising, then we could easily construct a table to give the details. The decision as to what comprised 'old' and 'young' would be arbitrary, but let us say we decided to analyse the situation by ten-year age-groups and then combine them later if we wanted. A table for this might then be shown as below.

How I learned about the play	Ages of respondents					
	To 24	25–34	35–44	45–54	55–64	65 & over
Newspaper advertisement						
Outdoor poster						
Playhouse mailing list						
Programme notes						
Indoor notice/poster						
From a friend						
From a relative						
Don't know						
Other means						
Total						

This sort of table is likely to be the end-product of a survey, and it is from the distribution of answers to questions set out in such tables that conclusions on the hypotheses will be made. Tables of this type make it clear to all readers on what grounds the writer is drawing conclusions. Statements such as 'the bulk of young people learned about the play from formal advertisements' are then referrable back to the original data which show clearly what these things mean in numerical terms. It is sometimes said by critics of surveys that by giving respondents answer categories to tick against some people are led to tick answers they would not have thought of for themselves. There is some truth in this. I have seen a survey of book reading in which respondents were asked to tick against a list of titles all those that they had read. The list contained one title which was entirely spurious, yet some people ticked it. In my own survey of visitors to the British Museum a few people, one week, claimed to have visited a gallery that had been temporarily closed. Every sensible survey designer accepts, in all humility, that his or her survey will never be perfect since survey respondents are not universally saints or geniuses; but at least the survey worker, in humility, *is* attempting to refine and improve the data collecting methods. This is surely preferable to stating, as I have seen students do in examinations, that 'all working-class children in Britain are alienated from the educational system', without a scrap of evidence being produced to back up this sweeping generalization.

Careful survey work requires a great deal of attention to be given to decisions about how questions are asked and how answers are categorized. It also requires the surveyor to think carefully about how interview schedules and/or questionnaires can be dealt with in bulk. Market research companies are accustomed to dealing with samples in their thousands which must be analysed very quickly to satisfy the requirements of the clients who are paying for the research to be done. In non-commercial and academic research there is rarely the pressure to produce complete reports within two weeks of a survey ending, but even so, the longer it takes to produce results, the more dated are those results when (or even, if) they eventually do appear in print. Some academic research seems virtually historical when one compares the date of the fieldwork and that of publication. Clearly what is needed, in addition to good planning of questions and answer categories, is some means of dealing rapidly with hundreds, perhaps thousands, of questionnaires or interview schedules. This can only be done if one accepts the overwhelming need for standardization of answers: that is, a clear categorization of responses which will enable them to be dealt with impersonally and mechanically, or electronically. When I say 'impersonally' I mean that the questionnaires *must* be amenable to analysis by people who have not been involved in the survey itself and who will not be required to interpret answers. Depth interviews of a very personal kind, with a very small number of people, may be interpreted qualitatively as well as quantitatively by the people who carried them out, but no one can sit down and consider hundreds of questionnaires in this way. The social survey measures. Sometimes it measures simple things such as age or marital status, sometimes it measures quite sophisticated things such as people's knowledge, preferences and attitudes. But whatever it measures it must do it in a standardized way — an elastic yardstick is no use to anyone.

ANALYSIS BY HAND SORTING

In these days of sophisticated data analysis procedures it may seem old-fashioned to suggest that a lot of survey analysis can still be done quite sensibly by simple hand sorting. By this I refer to what is sometimes called the 'tally' system of analysis. For example, suppose that you decided you wanted to know what proportions of books borrowed on a certain day from a local branch library were fiction and what were non-fiction. It might be that this information could be provided by a computer if the library uses a computer-based issue system. But let us suppose the library concerned is a 'mobile' library — a large van or trailer with no such fancy equipment. Each book borrowed is marked, either on the spine or inside, to show clearly whether it is fiction or non-fiction. If the assistant issueing the books has by his or her side a simple two-column sheet headed 'Fiction' and 'Non-fiction', all he or she needs to do, as the day progresses, is to 'tally' each book loaned according to category. Using the conventional 'five-barred gate' system, the result would be something like this:

Fiction	Non-fiction
⊦⊦⊦⊦ ⊦⊦⊦⊦ ⊦⊦⊦⊦ ⊦⊦⊦⊦ ⊦⊦⊦⊦ ⊦⊦⊦⊦ ⊦⊦⊦⊦ ⊦⊦⊦⊦ ⊦⊦⊦⊦ ⦙⦙⦙	⊦⊦⊦⊦ ⊦⊦⊦⊦ ⊦⊦⊦⊦ ⊦⊦⊦⊦ ⊦⊦⊦⊦ ⊦⊦⊦⊦ ⦙⦙⦙⦙
Total 48	Total 34

Probably every one of us, at some stage in our lives, has carried out some sort of survey along these lines. Schoolchildren are often to be seen conducting traffic surveys near their schools and tallying motor cars, lorries, vans, buses, and so on. Even at this very elementary level there is a procedure to be followed.

1 Define your terms. For example, what is a 'van', a 'bus', a 'lorry'? Is a private coach the same as a bus? Is a removal van a van or a lorry?
2 Observe your data. Decide where to survey and how to do it. Consider whether your sample is representative of a population.
3 Record your observations. Put down on paper your symbols (tally marks) which represent defined categories. Do your definitions work?
4 Analyse your results. Add up your tally marks. If you have been able to record without difficulty then this stage is simple.

I have deliberately spelled out this seemingly simple procedure in detail because, no matter how sophisticated one may become in analysis procedures, the basic nature of categorization does not alter. A piece of data, an observation, a book, a vehicle, is either one thing or another; in analysis work it cannot be both. Also, it should not be neither if the results are going to be comprehensive. For example, the suggested categorization of 'fiction' and 'non-fiction' begs the question of whether children's books will be included in the survey, and so categorized, or alternatively, excluded from the survey entirely because the survey is limited to adult loans only. There is no God-given right or wrong answer about these things — the survey designer must think in advance of all the possibilities and define categories appropriately for the job that is to be done. If the surveyor can do this effectively then simple surveys which do not require a lot of cross-tabulation (analysing one variable by another variable) may be analysed quite happily by simple hand sorting, using the tally system. A hundred questionnaires with a dozen questions, each question having up to five possible set answers does not require a main-frame computer for a simple straight count analysis. Twelve questions means twelve frequency distributions and every answer on every questionnaire will go into one box or another out of five for each question. Hundreds, probably thousands, of undergraduate (and even postgraduate) dissertations and theses must have incorporated surveys analysed by simple hand sorting using the tally system. This does not make their results any less valuable or valid than surveys analysed by more sophisticated means. The reason why we go on to mechanical and electronic means of analysis is that some survey data is too bulky and too complex to be sensibly done by hand. So, from the 'craftsman' hard analysis we move on to 'mass production' data analysis.

ANALYSIS BY PUNCH CARD

Although it is now out of date, it is interesting to consider the principles which lay behind one of the first mechanical means of data analysis. What was called the 'Cope-Chat' card, after its manufacturers, was a fairly simple means of analysing limited numbers of cases. The system was also used for information retrieval in offices and factories, but it was not uncommon to find it used for surveys of limited numbers and variables. The three items required were standard cards with circles punched out of them round the edges, hole-punchers rather like those used by ticket collecters on the railway and rods, very like knitting needles, for sorting. Each answer to a question would be given a number and by certain combinations four holes could be used for up to nine possible answers. Thus, the case of marital status could be dealt with by designating 1 = Single, 2 = Married, 3 = Widowed and 4 = Divorced. But if one wanted nine age categories then the numbers 5 to 9 could be obtained by punching more than one of the four holes: punching $4 + 1 = 5$, $4 + 2 = 6$, $4 + 3 = 7$, $4 + 3 + 1 = 8$ and $4 + 3 + 2 = 9$. Each questionnaire would then have to have its answers 'coded' so that it could be transformed into a punch card. When all the cards had been punched they could be put into a box, making sure they were all facing the same way and were the same way up. If we wanted to know, for example, how many people were married — and this was coded as '2' on the first question — then we would put a rod through the whole pack of cards and lift them up. The cards coded 'married', i.e. '2', would have been punched so that the circle had become an open 'u'. These cards would not be lifted out by the rod, would remain in the base and could then be counted.

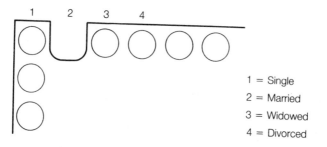

1 = Single
2 = Married
3 = Widowed
4 = Divorced

It is not difficult to see that this system is really better for a long-term filing system, say dealing with patients or customers or even stock, rather than more transitory survey data, but I have mentioned it out of more than purely historical interest because it introduces the principles of coding and sorting which underlie all subsequent developments.

Obviously, anyone using the above system would quickly begin to wish for a more sophisticated way of punching and sorting which would be less tedious in both procedures. This wish was fulfilled with the development of what were known at first as 'Powers-Samas', or 'Hollerith' cards, according to the manufacturer one used. Eventually this type of card became the monopoly of International Computers Limited and is today known by its initials as an 'ICL' card. Although even these cards have now given way to the use of magnetic tape or disks for storage for computer analysis they are still used by some survey workers and the principles upon which they work are helpful to us in understanding further modern developments. Although ICL cards can be produced in a variety of sizes the standard card is one with 80 'columns' on it, which means that it can deal with 80 quite separate sets of information. It is easiest to think of this as 80 separate questions which all have a 'column' each. Each column can be punched in 12 different places, and this actually means that a hole is knocked out of the card at one of 12 predetermined places on the column. So we may say that for 80 questions we can have up to 12 different answers for each question.

Let us now consider how a real-life example of a question and its answers can be turned into a column on a punch card. In the theatre surveys previously referred to, respondents were asked to tick one box which indicated their age-group. Nine possible answers were available.

In which age-group are you?

Under 11 ☐	19–24 ☐	45–54 ☐
11–14 ☐	25–34 ☐	55–64 ☐
15–18 ☐	35–44 ☐	65 and over ☐

These response categories cover all age possibilities and no sensible respondent can tick more than one, though a person might forget to tick or delibeately abstain from answering the question, so it will be wise to have a category for 'no answer'. We thus have ten possible answers altogether and we can 'code' them as:

1 = Under 11	4 = 19–24	7 = 45–54	0 = No answer
2 = 11–14	5 = 25–34	8 = 55–64	
3 = 15–18	6 = 35–44	9 = 65 and over	

The standard ICL card, a facsimile of which is shown on page 206, has 80 columns and each column can be used for up to twelve different separate answers. Each column, as can be seen, is numbered 0 and 1 to 9, but there is space above the 0 for two more 'codes', often designated 'Y' and 'X'. Our age question will use up ten of the 12 possible codes in whatever column it is placed. Let us imagine that the age question comes fairly late in the survey and is allocated to column 54. If a particular questionnaire then comes from a person aged 39, who has ticked the 35–44 age box, then for that questionnaire, as it is turned into a punch card, column 54 will be punched as a code 6 and that particular column will look like this:

Column 54

```
(Y)
(X)
 0
 1
 2
 3
 4
 5
[6]   (An actual rectangle would be punched out of the card to
 7    indicate code 6.)
 8
 9
```

ICL 4-353

PRINTED IN U.K.

If, for this survey, 62 columns were used for the coding of the answers to questions, then each questionnaire would end up as a punch card with rectangles punched out in each column from 1 to 62, with columns 63 to 80 unused and therefore unpunched.

The compilation of the 'code book' for a survey is a matter which demands careful thought and scrupulous attention to detail since the coding determines the analysis categories which form the basis of the resultant statistical tables. When the code book has been devised it should be possible to hand it, together with all the questionnaires, over to a coder who has had nothing to do with the fieldwork at all. If the coder has to keep coming back with questions such as 'How do I code "student" as an occupational category for Colum 48?' or 'Column 63 has codes for "Asia" and "the Near East"; in which should I code Israel?', then something is wrong.

Once a completed questionnaire has been fully coded all the answers will have been transformed into numbers and these numbers can then be punched, by means of specially designed machines, onto the blank cards. Thus, a complete questionnaire with 62 answers of all sorts becomes one punch card with holes in it on 62 columns. A pack of such cards can then be sorted on a machine which is also equipped with counters for each code (and this, not surprisingly, is called a counter-sorter). At a rate of about 1,000 cards a minute on a good machine the cards can be sorted, column by column, and the numbers in each code read off from the registers. If you want to analyse a particular question by sex then all you need do is to put the pack of cards through the counter-sorter at the appropriate column for sex and, as each code has a box into which cards can be directed as they are sorted, you get two packs of cards — one for males, the other for females. You then put each pack through the counter-sorter for whatever other column you want to analyse and the result is two sets of data for comparison.

Counter-sorters are now hard to find as they were made

rapidly obsolete by the development of smaller computers, but I have deliberately described the way they worked because, first, one could actually *see* what was happening with them and second, the process of rigid categorization which was developed for punch-card analysis lies at the heart of the principles used in applying computers to survey analysis. It is still possible to use punch cards with modern main-frame computers, though it is now much more common for the punchers to put the data onto electronic tape or disks, which are easier to handle and store. The enormous advantage of the computer is the vast amount of data which it can handle at extraordinarily high speed.

SURVEYS AND COMPUTERS

There are today literally hundreds of books on the use of computers and this is not the place to try to cover the enormous range of use to which computers of all sizes can be put.[1] However, there is a danger of computers being seen as masters rather than servants and it is therefore important to note that computers — even the most advanced ones — can only do what they have been told to do. The instructions contained in program can range from a simple houehold budget to a complex space programme.

The whole operation begins with human beings, who 'input' data into a central processing unit, which then 'outputs' results by way of printed sheets, words on screens, department-store receipts, and so on. Computers have perhaps appeared to take on human characteristics because of the use of the word 'language' to describe the codes by which instructions can be given to a computer. BASIC is a language now well known to thousands of owners of home computers, but it is not an ordinary language, it is an agreed means of putting data into a format which can be dealt with by a computer. A computer has no 'brain'; it has to have data fed into it in a special way by means of a recognized code.

The input console used for inputting resembles a complex typewriter keyboard which contains both 'alpha' and 'numeric' symbols. Once the computer has been programmed to understand a particular language, the keyboard characters can be used in the ordinary way as letters or numbers, and thus one can input, for example, one's own name, simply by typing it in. (This is done by means of electrical impulses using the binary system. Every character, called a 'byte', put into the computer is made up of binary digits or 'bits' which are understood by the computer.)

Before the central processing unit can do anything at all with the data inputted it must have a program which instructs it in what to do. On introductory courses in computing beginners are frequently bemused by the complexity involved in simply instructing the computer to do the simplest tasks of addition or subtraction. Happily for social survey workers, many of the jobs they want done by computers are fairly straightforward and not really very difficult to program. Survey analysis frequently involves a need for frequency distributions, cross tabulations, calculations of averages, standard deviations, and so on. For large computers such tasks can be carried out in the blink of an eye for hundreds or even thousands of cases.

Short cuts to avoid writing completely new programs for each survey are made by means of a Statistical Package for the Social Sciences (SPSS), which is a general outline program which can be adapted reasonably easily for each particular survey (or each different customer). Survey workers who would themselves never become proper programers can learn to use the SPSS for themselves. Results can be printed, with percentages alongside the raw data, and measures of central tendency and dispersion will accompany the tables. Such is the attraction of these print-outs that it is not uncommon for surveyors to be charmed into asking for extra cross-tabulations — which can be produced so quickly — and the result can then be a monster pile of paper which only a person, rather than a machine, can read. Another simple package for survey data is called MINITAB. With this the survey workers can produce frequency distributions, histograms and not-too-complicated cross-tabulations at the keyboard without having to work out a full program in advance. Both SPSS and MINITAB are available in the UK and USA and computer centre staff will advise survey workers about them.

The computer's worth in survey work is beyond doubt. However, one or two words of caution may not go amiss. First, a computer demands accuracy from the input. As the saying goes, 'Garbage in — garbage out', except that often nothing comes out at all. Survey workers (in my humble opinion) get the best value from computers by learning to work *with* the computing staff (I am leaving aside here the use of personal and mini-computers, which can be useful for some analysis, but which are often limited in their application in any large-scale surveys). To work with computing people means to be precise and accurate in all things — a trait not always found in all social scientists. Also, programing means being clear *in advance* as to what one wants the computer to do. With the old-fashioned punch cards and counter-sorters part of the fun was getting an unexpected result on a run through a column and deciding there and then that perhaps it would be interesting to see if this arose from differences of sex, age, or social class. For the computer program the decision needs to be made in advance; you can, of course, come back again and again to the computer, but computer programers, not surprisingly, do not always react kindly to re-writing a program three times a week.

Perhaps the best advice one can give to a social survey worker these days is to read a basic text, preferably a *very* simple one, on how main-frame computers work, and get a bit of what is called 'hands on' experience and then make sure that you approach your friendly computer programer very early on in your questionnaire planning so that you end up working together, not against each other. If you can also gain experience with personal and/or mini-computers this can only be to the good in extending your understanding of a very valuable modern analysis tool.

PRESENTATION OF RESULTS

Some people, especially undergraduates working on their first survey, worry about whether they are asking their informants for enough information. These people usually finish up at the analysis stage wondering what to do with the masses of information they have collected. It cannot be stressed too much or too often that no information should be collected simply for the sake of information collecting. The factor of relevance becomes very clearly apparent at the stage when the research report is to be written up. So often a thesis or dissertation contains a very large appendix of 'supplementary tables' and the experienced eye quickly sees that what this really means is that 'I collected all this information and I really don't know what to do with it since it really isn't relevant to the point of my thesis, so I'll stick it in an appendix rather than throw it away and perhaps it will impress my examiner.'

Tables of results are compiled to make a point, not to make padding. If they have a job to do and a valid reason for existing they are likely to find a place in the text rather than in an appendix. This is not to say that appendices are all just rubbish dumps — this would be quite misleading — but there is a difference between an appendix which contains a highly detailed discussion on sampling, or a special form of significance testing which would hold up to the flow of the main argument, and the appendix which simply contains all those tables which were left over when the narrative had been written.

Let us, therefore, look at the form which a research report may take. Opinions differ widely about points of detail in presenting research findings so what follows must be a personal view. It seems to me that in all writing, from a first-year undergraduate essay through to Ph.D. thesis there is a similar pattern for presentation. This can be put very briefly indeed in three stages:

1 Say what you intend to write about.
2 Write about it.
3 Come to a conclusion.

If we take it that (1) is the introduction in which the problem is briefly but clearly stated and that (3) is the drawing together of the threads, which should not be a complete re-statement of all that has already been said, then neither (1) nor (3) need be very long. This leaves (2) as the main part of the writing, and this can be sub-divided into a number of sections. I have made it clear in earlier pages that I consider that a sociological study, as opposed to a merely social one, stems from some theoretical or conceptual starting point. If this is so then it is important that the writer makes plain what the starting point is. This, then, is what we will call the theoretical introduction, and since it comes from theory it is necessary to explain clearly what the theory is and what work has already been done in this field. From this general consideration the writer may then go on to a more detailed consideration of the particular piece of work which he is about to attempt. This means that he will be looking in much greater detail at a more limited field of study, will go into more detail in the theory and will introduce other people's researches where appropriate. From this stage the researcher will then be able to develop his own hypotheses and the reader will follow through the particular line of thought and appreciate what is to be done and why. At this stage the writer will develop his own empirical ideas and the actual enquiry to be carried out will be outlined, with the relevance of the enquiry never in doubt. Whether the enquiry is to include a sample survey or whether it never goes outside the library does not really matter, since the writer will be presenting data which he has collected to test the thesis being put forward. The next stage is the description of the means used to collect the data and this will lead on to the presentation of the data themselves, organized in a form appropriate to the needs of the study. If these results are clearly presented, always being used to illustrate and illuminate the points of the hypotheses, then they will tell their own story and the conclusions need only be relatively brief.

It will be seen that this programme is based on the idea of 'flow' which comes from one section leading naturally into the next. If the research is properly thought out and planned the naturalness will be there. If the research has been badly planned and not adequately thought out in advance then the natural flow will be replaced by a jerky progression which will show where the parts fail to fit together properly. The research which is good to read, clearly presented and satisfying in its results, does not just happen out of the blue — the 10 per cent inspiration must be built around and supported by the 90 per cent perspiration.

It will be seen that the above outline also helps the researcher to clarify the relationship between his own research and that of the general field in which he is working. Since any one research project can only contribute a very little to the advancement of total knowledge it is especially important for beginners to recognize the need to scale down their enquiries to a size which will result in a useful special contribution, rather than trying to re-write, let us say, the whole of industrial sociology in one three-year project. Sociologists are very often, by the very nature of their interests, 'big' in their thinking. No one would want sociology to become suffocated in detail; but complex structures (such as bodies of theory) are made up from well constructed small parts (and the major developments in the natural sciences have come from an understanding of minutely small things, such as chromosomes and particles). The small piece of research, well done, is very satisfying to the doer and is often of more real value in the end than the big project badly done. Small can be very beautiful.

Notes

Chapter 1 THE STUDY OF SOCIAL BEHAVIOUR

1 Taken from Morris Ginsberg, *Sociology*, Oxford, 1934.
2 Charles Booth, *Life and Labour of the People of London*, London, 1902-4; B. Seebohm Rowntree, *Poverty, a Study of Town Life*, London, 1902.
3 See Peter Townsend, *The Concept of Poverty*, London, 1970; and *Poverty in the United Kingdom*, London, 1979.

Chapter 2 SCIENTIFIC METHOD AND SOCIAL RESEARCH

1 Karl Pearson, *The Grammar of Science*, London, 1900.
2 See Dorothy Davis, *A History of Shopping*, London, 1966, for interesting examples of lack of standardization in the retail trades in the eighteenth and nineteenth centuries.
3 G. Lundberg, *Social Research*, London, 1948. Lundberg has been criticized by subjectivist sociologists for his so-called 'positivist' approach, which often indicates a lack of understanding of and sympathy for scientific method on the part of his critics.
4 The Market Research Society also has a five-point scale based on occupational prestige which is now commonly accepted and used in most market research surveys.
5 Sidney and Beatrice Webb, *Methods of Social Study*, London, 1932. It is not without interest that this aspect of the Webbs' work is now relatively forgotten by students who still refer to their more political activities.

Chapter 3   BASIC STEPS IN SOCIAL RESEARCH

1 See particularly W.I.B. Beveridge, *The Art of Scientific Investigation*, London, 1951, for some interesting examples.
2 Elton Mayo, *The Human Problems of an Industrial Civilisation*, Boston, 1946.
3 E. Gellner, in S.J. Gould and W.A. Kolb (eds), *A Dictionary of the Social Sciences*, London, 1964.
4 M. Shipman, *The Limitations of Social Research*, London, 1981.
5 D. Caradog Jones, *The Social Survey of Merseyside*, London, 1934.
6 Margaret Hagood, *Statistics for Sociologists*, New York, 1947.
7 M. Young and P. Willmott, *Family and Kinship in East London*, London, 1957.
8 E.R. Wickham, *Church and People in an Industrial City*, London, 1957.

Chapter 4   DOCUMENTARY SOURCES OF DATA

1 See either P. Quennell (ed), *Mayhew's London*, London, n.d., or John L. Bradley (ed.), *Selections from London Labour and the London Poor*, London, 1965, for samples from Mayhew's reports. See also E.P. Thompson and Eileen Yeo, *The Unknown Mayhew*, Harmondsworth, 1973, for an excellent appraisal of Mayhew as an early sociologist as well as journalist.
2 John Madge, *The Tools of Social Science*, London, 1953, and L. Gottschalk, C. Kluckholn and R.C. Angell, *The Use of Personal Documents in History, Anthropology and Sociology*, New York, 1945. The latter is a classic statement on this topic.
3 My italics. *The Observer*, 5 November 1961.
4 The finest example of this is to be found in George Orwell's novel *Nineteen Eighty-four*, in which the central character's occupation is the re-writing of history.
5 Another fascinating example of the inaccuracy of recorded history is to be found in Josephine Tey's detective story *The Daughter of Time* (1951), where a British detective investigates the character of Richard III and the mystery of the murder of the Princes in the Tower.
6 Harold Evans, *Newsman's English*, London, 1972.
7 David Thomson, *England in the Twentieth Century*, Harmondsworth, 1965.
8 Peter H. Mann, *Students and Books*, London, 1974.
9 See *The Diary of Anne Frank*, London, 1968, and Chaim A.

Kaplan, *Scroll of Agony: The Warsaw Diaries of Chaim A. Kaplan*, London, 1966.

10 W.I. Thomas and F. Znaniecki, *The Polish Peasant in Europe and America*, New York, 1927. This is a classic of its kind.

11 Royal Commission on the Housing of the Working Classes (1885), *Minutes of Evidence*, p. 305, Q. 9157.

12 Ibid., p. 299, Q. 9004.

13 E. Moberly Bell, *Octavia Hill, a Biography*, London, 1946. For my own assessment see Peter H. Mann 'Octavia Hill: an Appraisal', *Town Planning Review*, vol. 23, no. 3, October, 1952.

14 A review article in *The Observer*, 23 July, 1961.

15 In *Time and Tide*, a weekly journal, 15 October 1957.

16 Herbert Blumer, *An Appraisal of Thomas and Znaniecki's 'The Polish peasant in Europe and America'*, New York, 1939.

17 Gustav Jahoda, 'Adolescent Attitudes to Starting Work', *Occupational Psychology*, vol. 23, no. 3, July 1949.

18 Peter H. Mann, 'Young People's Attitudes to Bookselling', *Bookseller*, 10 July 1971.

19 Arthur Marwick, *The Nature of History*, London, 1970.

20 E.H. Carr, *What is History?*, London, 1961.

21 G.R. Elton, *The Practice of History*, Sydney University Press, 1967.

22 See first an article by A.E. Ashworth, 'The Sociology of Trench Warfare 1914–18', *British Journal of Sociology*, vol. 9, 1968, and also his book *Trench Warfare 1914–18*, London, 1980.

23 Martin L. Ward, *Readers and Library Users*, London, 1977.

24 An invaluable guide to the use of bibliographical sources for social scientists is Colin Harris, *Social Welfare Information: a Guide to Sources*, published by Newcastle Polytechnic in 1978 as part of a library instruction package.

Chapter 5   PEOPLE AS SOURCES OF DATA

1 For the pioneer articles on this work see Peter H. Mann, 'Surveying a Theatre Audience: Methodological Problems', *British Journal of Sociology*, vol. 13, no. 4, December 1966, and 'Surveying a Theatre Audience: Findings', *British Journal of Sociology*, vol. 18, no. 1, March 1967.

2 J.J. Hader and E.C. Lindeman, *Dynamic Social Research*, London, 1933.

3 John Madge, *The Tools of Social Science*, London, 1953.

4 William F. Whyte, *Street Corner Society*, Chicago, 1949.

5 Robert and Helen Lynd, *Middletown* and *Middletown in Transition*, New York, 1929 and 1937.
6 John Howard Griffin, *Black Like Me*, London, 1960.
7 Tony Wilkinson, *Down and Out*, London, 1981.
8 Peter Keating (ed.), *Into Unknown England, 1866–1913*, London, 1976.
9 Ronald Blythe, *Akenfield*, Harmondsworth, 1969.

Chapter 6   THE SAMPLE SURVEY WITH FORMAL INTERVIEWS

1 M. Schofield, *The Sexual Behaviour of Young Adults*, Harmondsworth, 1973.
2 C.A. Moser, *Survey Methods in Social Investigation*, London, 1958.
3 A.L. Bowley, *Elements of Statistics*, 6th edn, London, 1946.

Chapter 7   THE SELF-COMPLETED QUESTIONNAIRE

1 In addition to theatre audiences I also surveyed audiences for orchestral concerts using the same techniques, and these were equally successful. See Arts Council of Great Britain, *A Report on Orchestral Resources in Great Britain*, Appendix 1, London, 1970.
2 The same problem is also being experienced by public librarians who apparently receive far too many questionnaires from librarianship students carrying out individual projects.
3 R.K. Kelsall, *Women and Teaching*, HMSO, London, 1963.
4 The main problem with this sample was to try to get them to reply *quickly*. Some replies came in months after the mailing.

Chapter 8   HOW TO ASK QUESTIONS

1 It is interesting that an interview-based study of children's reading habits revealed much wider reading of rather unpleasant horror and occult books than had been expected. In a large-scale enquiry previously made by self-completed questionnaires there had been little indication of such reading.
2 Interestingly, I used a questionnaire for this very purpose after writing these lines. I was staying in an expensive hotel overnight and the service was very poor, so I used a questionnaire (which I would otherwise probably not have completed) for the express purpose of listing my criticisms.

Chapter 9   ANALYSIS AND PRESENTATION OF RESULTS

1 I strongly recommend the Ladybird book by David Carey *How it works . . . The Computer*, Loughborough, 1979, as a brilliantly clear introduction to the principles of computing. For learning to use a microcomputer probably the *30 hour Basic* handbook to be used with the BBC computer is the most helpful of many handbooks on the market.

Index